Touching Heaven

Touching Heaven

REAL STORIES of CHILDREN, LIFE, and ETERNITY

Leanne Hadley

Revell

a division of Baker Publishing Group
Grand Rapids, Michigan

Published by Revell
a division of Baker Publishing Group
P.O. Box 6287, Grand Rapids, MI 49516-6287
www.revellbooks.com

Printed in the United States of America

Library of Congress Cataloging-in-Publication Data
Hadley, Leanne Ciampa.
    Touching heaven : real stories of children, life, and eternity / Leanne Hadley.
      pages cm
    ISBN 978-0-8007-2171-8 (pbk.)
    1. Children—Death—Religious aspects—Christianity. I. Title.
BV4907.H28 2013
242′.4—dc23   2012050048

Unless otherwise indicated, Scripture quotations are from the King James Version of the Bible.

Scripture quotations labeled NIV are from the Holy Bible, New International Version®. NIV®. Copyright © 1973, 1978, 1984, 2011 by Biblica, Inc.™ Used by permission of Zondervan. All rights reserved worldwide. www.zondervan.com

The internet addresses, email addresses, and phone numbers in this book are accurate at the time of publication. They are provided as a resource. Baker Publishing Group does not endorse them or vouch for their content or permanence.

The stories in this book are based on individuals the author has met or known in real life, but specific details and personal characteristics have been altered or left out to honor privacy. Any resemblance to a specific real person the reader may know is purely coincidental.

13 14 15 16 17 18 19   7 6 5 4 3 2 1

To my sons, Julian and Britton, and to Janell, my three most beloved!

To Bobbie for all her teaching, support, and friendship, and for always wanting the best for me.

And lastly, to the many children at the hospital who were honest and brave and shared their truth with me. You taught me so much and strengthened my faith, and I will forever hold your precious souls close to my heart.

Contents

Acknowledgments

I would like to thank the staff of Baker Publishing Group for guiding me through the process of writing this book with such professionalism and sensitivity. I especially thank Andrea Doering, who has journeyed with me and guided me every step of the way. I am certain that without her urging and support I would not have written this book. My words cannot express my gratitude.

I would also to thank my family and friends for their never-ending encouragement and faith in me, not only during the writing of this book, but in all times and all places. You know who you are, and I thank God for each of you!

Introduction

From the age of four, I imagined myself working with children. As soon as I was old enough, I began baby-sitting, helping out in the church nursery, visiting children at the Shriners hospitals for burned children, and doing physical therapy with children with cerebral palsy each Saturday morning. From that time on, I've worked with children, and I find them to be the most interesting and Spirit-filled people I know!

Jesus told those around him that unless they became like children, they would never enter the kingdom of heaven. I have found those words to be true. Children have much to teach the adults around them about God, faith, and what it means to be human. I know that children need to be taught well. They are not adults, and as such, they need instruction and schooling in matters of life and faith. However, I believe there is a balance between teaching them and at the same time respecting them enough to realize just how wise, insightful, and holy they already are.

When I was first approached to write this book about the experiences of children who were crossing over from this world into heaven, I wondered if I would be exploiting the sacred times we shared together. I wondered if writing about these experiences would in some way spoil the sacredness of the journey. I prayed hard about it and feel confident that these stories should be shared. While I do not understand why these precious little ones died when they did, or why their families had to endure the unique pain that comes with losing a child, these children have much to teach others about the dying process, heaven, and God.

Because I want to protect the identities of the children and their families, I have changed a few of the details of each story. Sometimes I chose to change the sex of the child or alter their age a bit, and, of course, I have used anonymous names. However, I have not changed the experiences they shared with me. Those were such blessed and holy times for me. I've done everything I can to relate them to you with honesty, sensitivity, and a deep respect and gratitude for being present during those children's journeys.

It is my prayer that this book will provide comfort because of its topic and will remind each of us of the importance of listening to the children around us every day. During our times with them, when we stop instructing and correcting them and instead start listening to them, we will discover that Jesus knew children well. Jesus knew how wise, insightful, and close to God they are. It is also my prayer that this book will inspire all of us to remember just how blessed we are to have children as a part of our lives, our society, and our world.

1

My Story of Faith-Filled Doubt

And when from death I'm free, I'll sing on, I'll sing on;
And when from death I'm free, I'll sing on.
And when from death I'm free, I'll sing and joyful be;
And through eternity, I'll sing on, I'll sing on;
And through eternity, I'll sing on.
    Alexander Means, *What Wondrous Love Is This?*

I was born during the last six weeks of my father's courses at seminary. He, my mother, and my sister Paula had been living in the steeple of a church in Denver, where he worked as a custodian so they could make a living during his time in school. So my first home was in the steeple of a church. Is it any wonder that I went into the ministry?

Six weeks after I was born, we moved "home" to Kentucky, where my dad spent the first years of his career serving the small churches of the Deep South. I grew up surrounded by church people, revivals, sermons, and hymns. Most of my childhood memories happened in whatever church my father was serving at the time.

I remember a couple coming to our home in the middle of the night asking my dad if he would marry them before the man left for Vietnam the following morning. My father did, and I watched, wearing my pajamas, from the steps going up to my room.

The first Christmas my father served as an associate minister, the senior minister and his wife gave me a fake fur muff to wear around my neck and put my hands in when I got cold. It was beautiful, but even better was the small angel ornament on the ribbon of the package. She had a head made of glass, and her body was made of some kind of netting and wire that had been dipped in gold. I hung her on my Christmas tree and imagined what it would have been like for an angel to tell Mary she was going to give birth to the Son of God.

I loved being the child of a minister. It was difficult at times with all the moving around and changing schools, but I knew that my place was in the church and that the church was where God could be experienced and felt as nowhere else.

The only times I felt closer to God than in the church were when I accompanied my father on his calls to church members. My dad didn't like me going along, but he had no choice. As soon as he mentioned he was going to make calls, I went upstairs, put on a Sunday dress, and announced that I would be coming with him.

Most of the people we would visit were old. I loved these people! I loved how their houses smelled, that they always offered me something to eat, and that they always told me how pretty I was in my Sunday dress and fancy shoes. I loved the stories they told and the perspective they had on life. Many of them laughed a lot and seemed to be much more honest than other adults I knew. They weren't, in my opinion, as full of themselves as others were. Many of them were ill, and they told me about God and not being afraid to die. I marveled at their courage and openness.

When these people died, I would accompany my dad to their funerals. I needed to be there to celebrate that these dear, brave people had crossed over into heaven. I met their families and always told them the things their loved ones had shared with me about not being afraid to die. I sat at their funerals and wondered why people were crying when death was simply going to be with God face-to-face.

My dad read Scriptures from his King James Bible, such as John 14:1–6:

> Let not your heart be troubled: ye believe in God, believe also in me. In my Father's house are many mansions: if it were not so, I would have told you. I go to prepare a place for you. And if I go and prepare a place for you, I will come again, and receive you unto myself; that where I am, there ye may be also. And whither I go ye know, and the way ye know.
>
> Thomas saith unto him, Lord, we know not whither thou goest; and how can we know the way?
>
> Jesus saith unto him, I am the way, the truth, and the life: no man cometh unto the Father, but by me.

I imagined these people I loved so dearly lying in their beds, about to die, and having Jesus himself come and take them to heaven. I tried to imagine what their new home must look like. I had piercing theological questions, such as, "Will they share a room in heaven like I have to share a room with my sister?" and "Will they be expected to keep their room clean and make their bed each day?" Surely not! It would be a happy and wonderful place where people sang all day and praised God all the time.

My thoughts about heaven were interrupted as the congregation started to sing the hymn "What Wondrous Love Is This?" My dad had it sung at nearly every funeral he officiated. It was by far my favorite hymn and still is today. I remember how it began slowly and quietly, and as each verse continued, it would build, until the last verse, when I would be singing at the top of my lungs:

> And when from death I'm free, I'll sing on, I'll sing on;
> And when from death I'm free, I'll sing on.
> And when from death I'm free, I'll sing and joyful be;
> And through eternity, I'll sing on, I'll sing on;
> And through eternity, I'll sing on.

I would sing every word because I believed every word. Death was not an ending of our lives but the beginning of our time with God!

Funerals for me were not sad or distressing but times to think about God, heaven, and life after death, and I had no fear, no doubt, and no worries. For many children, this is the case. They are fascinated with death rather than fearful of it, because, as psychologists tell us, young children cannot really understand the permanence of death. However true this might be, I did understand death was forever. But during the time of forever, you were with God in that wonderful house with a room all to yourself and a bed you never had to make!

For preachers' kids, death is a huge part of life. There is no way to shelter them from funerals. We lived in a parsonage right next to the church. The funeral hearse came and went. My dad was called to get out of bed in the middle of the night and go to the hospital or home where a church member was dying, and he wrote his eulogies at the kitchen table while my mom kept us busy and quiet in the other room. Death was simply a part of my everyday life.

The first time I realized death wasn't simply a happy time of celebration was when I was nine years old. I was in bed and woke up because the phone in the hall was ringing. My mother answered it, and all I remember is her scream, which scared me. It's still the saddest noise I've ever heard. The next thing I knew, she flipped on the light switch in our bedroom and told my sister and me to pack three play-clothes outfits and a Sunday dress and shoes. No one told me, but from the deep distress on my mother's face, I just knew my granny had died.

We drove the rest of the night back home to Kentucky, and when we got to Granny and Pa's house, no one greeted us at the car as they always had in the past. We went up the tall stairs to their front porch, and I was still about five steps from the top when I heard my pa crying. I started to cry too and realized that death was complex, sad, and not quite the joyful experience I had thought it to be.

The three days we spent in Kentucky were some of the saddest of my life. I approached the casket at the visitation and saw my granny. She was dressed in a pink nightgown and looked so pretty. Her hair was perfect and she was wearing lipstick, something she rarely wore. I knew that I was seeing only her body. Her soul was now with God in heaven. But I missed her body, her hugs, her laughter, and her kisses. I wanted her body to have its soul back. I wanted my granny to come home, not to the heavenly home but to her home on earth. It was a sad time, though I never doubted my granny had gone to heaven and lived with God.

When I was in high school, I read *On Death and Dying* by Elisabeth Kübler-Ross. The book described her work with dying people, many of whom were children. I was fascinated by each account in the book and by her work. I decided then and there that I would work with the dying the rest of my life. I thought I would become a child psychologist or nurse, but God had other plans, and I decided—or maybe God decided—that I should serve the dying as a minister.

I took that confidence with me to college, to be confronted for the first time in my life with people who didn't share my faith-filled background. I met wonderful people at college, including many professors, who were professed atheists. I took a class called "God and Society," thinking it would be a Bible study about where God is in our world. Instead, it was a class where we read the writings of famous atheists who challenged the very idea that God was even present in the world, because, as they believed, God did not exist. Their main reasons for doubting the existence of God were that death was cruel and unfair and that children died before they had the chance to grow up.

For the first time in my life, I doubted. I didn't leave God behind, stop praying, or stop going to church, but deep inside me was a little piece of doubt about the size of a corn kernel. It wasn't huge and it wasn't cause for me to give up my hopes of becoming a minister, but it didn't belong there, and it bothered me.

When I started seminary classes and began imagining myself as a minister or a chaplain, I was haunted by that kernel of doubt. Could I really preach sermons about God and have this doubt in my heart? Did that make me a fake? How could I sit at people's bedsides and promise them that they would be okay after death, that they had nothing to fear, if I had this doubt myself? Would I be a liar?

I will never forget the moment I almost left the seminary altogether. I was sitting in our mandatory weekly chapel service, and the hymn following the sermon was "What Wondrous Love Is This?" I was excited we would be singing my all-time favorite hymn and looked forward to it the entire service.

We began singing, and just as it had always been during my childhood, the song began slowly, and as each verse progressed, the organ began to swell, causing the people to sing louder. By the last verse, everyone was singing at the top of their lungs—except for me. I was crying. That kernel of doubt was lodged in my soul, and I could not sing those words. I no longer believed them with my whole heart. I was uncertain if I had any song to sing for God, whom I had believed in so deeply my entire life and now doubted. It wasn't huge doubt, but it was there, and it made me sick, lonely, ashamed, and uncertain about my call to ministry.

I considered leaving the seminary that very day, but I was unsure how to tell my parents, who were so thrilled that I was choosing to follow in my father's footsteps and to answer God's call. I decided to stay one semester and see if my doubt might fade.

That same day, all the first-year students were invited to a series of interviews as we tried to find a field-ministry placement. We were given a list of churches and agencies that were willing to have interns. We had to select our top five choices and then were assigned interview times with each of them. I placed a check mark beside my top five choices but really wanted one only position—as a student chaplain to dying children at a children's hospital. I was on pins and needles waiting to hear if I had been chosen. I cannot tell you how blessed I felt to be selected as one of three chaplains to work at the hospital.

The night before I started, I prayed to God, admitting my sin of doubt and asking him with all my heart to give me more faith and to shatter my doubts. I was hoping for an experience much like Moses—I imagined a burning bush outside my window would shatter my fear. Or maybe a vision like Ezekiel was given would do the job. Or perhaps a moment when my heart would be strangely warmed, like John Wesley. Nothing happened that night, so I went to work, excited but disappointed my prayer had not been answered.

Little did I know that God would answer my prayer and my doubts would disappear as I spent time with the children at the hospital. They were not theologians or learned scholars or saints. They were simply children who were facing their own deaths and were open and honest about what they were experiencing.

I was a young woman who had just turned twenty-two and knew nothing about being a chaplain, and we didn't have a long training period before we were allowed to visit the kids. Luckily Toni, the sole chaplain for the hospital for years, was my supervisor. Her style was unique and trusting. She simply gave us a badge that read "Student Chaplain" and told us to go visit some kids and meet with her when we were done. We would meet in what we called the outer office, which was a small area where there were vending machines and two booths to sit in.

I worked at the hospital all three years while I was in seminary, and during those three years my prayer was answered. When I finally finished working at the hospital, I no longer doubted whether heaven was real, and I once again believed in God with the faith I'd had as a child.

My faith teachers were the children. Though I was a chaplain, I rarely had the words to make their deaths easier, nor did I feel my expressions of comfort were all that compelling to them. All I really did was visit them, listen to them, and learn from them about God, heaven, and what dying is like. And these young people, from ages four to fifteen, taught me the realities of God.

It has been many years since I worked at that hospital, but I recall the faces and the conversations I had with these children like it was yesterday. They were some of the most spiritual and profound experiences of my life. I'm writing this book to share their stories with you so that you too can learn about eternity from the best teachers there are.

Jesus said, "See that you do not despise one of these little ones. For I tell you that their angels in heaven always see the face of my Father in heaven" (Matt. 18:10 NIV). It is my experience that these children, who bravely faced their deaths and were willing to share about their experiences, had angels who saw God's face. They have much to teach us all about what death is really like.

Not only do I believe these children's angels saw the face of God, but I also believe that as they died, the children themselves saw the face of God. The word *angel* in Greek means "messenger," and for me, these children were messengers of God, sharing hope, love, and light in the face of death.

During my years as a student chaplain, I met hundreds of children. Most of them got better and went home. Some of them died and went home to God. I learned lessons from nearly all of the children I visited, but there were some whose journey from this life to life eternal healed my doubt and increased my faith beyond measure. These stories are the ones I want to share with you. I will be forever grateful to these tiny teachers and am eager for you to hear their stories and learn their lessons.

2

Tommy

The main children's floor of the hospital was a rectangle. Patients' rooms were on the outside of the rectangle, and in the center were a nurses' station and a playroom where the kids could come and relax. The woman who ran the playroom was a play therapist named Katy. She was the same age as me, full of energy, and a delight. We became friends almost immediately, and I was always welcome to visit kids in the playroom. Her duties included using play therapy to help kids prepare for whatever they were facing. A child who was having surgery could use a play surgery kit and pretend to be a doctor and care for others. A child who needed to be in isolation could use a special doll to practice washing their hands and putting on a gown so that they could educate the adults who came to visit about the importance of both acts.

One day Katy asked me if I wanted to go with her while she helped a little boy with leukemia prepare for a bone marrow test. I agreed, and we went into the room of one of the most beautiful children I have ever seen. Tommy was four years old and sitting in the middle of his hospital bed. He was tiny for his age, and the bed made him seem even smaller. His mother told me he had curly blond hair before the chemotherapy, but he was bald by the time I met him. He had a large head, as many four-year-olds do, but he was thin and so it appeared to be extra large. He had on shorts but no shirt and had a port going into his chest to make it easier for him to receive the needed treatments.

As soon as he saw Katy, he smiled. It was clear that he liked her very much. She introduced me as her friend, and they spent time using puppets and plastic needles to talk about how getting a spinal tap is easier when you curl in a ball and hold very still. He played and laughed and then started to cry; he had had several spinal taps before and remembered how painful they were. I fell in love with this child right then, and he became one of the kids I never failed to visit each time I came into the hospital.

Tommy's mom was a single mother, very devoted to him. She ate every meal and spent every night in his room. She never left his side, for two reasons. The first is she felt guilty that Tommy was sick. In all the years I've worked with death and dying, I have never met a mother who didn't blame herself in some way for the illness or death of her child. I think it stems from the strong drive mothers have to protect their little ones, and when they get sick or die, mothers often assume responsibility for it.

Tommy's mom was one of those who assumed guilt for her child's illness. She had smoked marijuana as a young woman and was afraid that it had caused her child to get leukemia. The doctors assured her that was not the case, but she still felt guilt. She also worried because she had been raised in the church but had found it a judgmental place when she got pregnant as a teen. She left the church and had not gone back until her son became sick. She worried that God was punishing her for her lack of faithfulness.

The other reason that Tommy's mother never left his side was because he became anxious whenever she would leave his room. He would cry, jump on the bed, and tear the sheets off. Sometimes he would try to take his IV lines out or disconnect his heart monitor. His mother could not stand to see him so upset, and the staff had little time to sit with him while she left. She had family, but they lived out of town and were not at the hospital often enough to make her leaving part of Tommy's routine. So day after day, hour after hour, she sat next to her child.

Tommy was dying—but he was one of the most life-filled children I have ever met. He loved to play, laugh, and do puzzles, and he had a large vocabulary for such a young child. He was also ornery and loved to play tricks. Often he would hide in the bathroom or under his bed waiting for a staff member to come in. Then he would jump out and cackle because he had scared them!

When I entered his room, his first words were always, "Did you bring me a new toy?" He said this to everyone. He knew the answer would be no most of the time, but he continued to ask and then would make a dramatic sad face and pout. After about five seconds, he would start to smile, laugh his little laugh, and invite whoever was visiting to play with a toy he already had.

It is difficult to describe Tommy because he was a rather naughty boy, but in a wonderful, full-of-life, four-year-old way. He wasn't naughty or ornery because he was bad but because he was full of excitement, lacking inhibition, and bored from spending so many days in the hospital. He didn't feel well, but he never complained about that.

Once when I went in to visit him, he had been to the gift shop and was very sad. His big blue eyes were brimming with tears. He explained to me that his grandmother had sent him a card with ten dollars in it, and he wanted to buy a new toy at the gift shop, so his mom had taken him there. I could see that he was upset, and I felt bad because I knew how expensive things in the gift shop sometimes were. I assumed that he hadn't had enough money to buy the toy he wanted, but that wasn't the case at all.

"I went to the gift shop with my ten dollars and looked at every toy there, and there wasn't a single toy in there that I didn't already have," Tommy said. "And now Mommy won't take me to the toy store!"

I explained that he wasn't allowed to leave the hospital because his blood counts were so low. He still wanted a new toy and told his sad tale to everyone who visited that day. I have no idea how many staff members went to the toy store that night, but I do know that when I visited the next day, he had several new toys sitting on his bed, including the one I had bought.

One day the Special Wish woman came to the hospital. The Special Wish Foundation's mission is to grant wishes to children with a life-threatening illness. Tommy was thrilled to be able to have a wish granted. The only problem was that he couldn't decide on just one wish. He had three wishes that he—and I quote—"really, really, really, really, really, really" wanted! He sat there with a worried look on his face, about to cry because the stress of deciding was so intense and he couldn't decide. The woman explained that the foundation could grant only one wish, so Tommy needed to think about it and let her know what his most special wish would be.

For days he stressed over which wish to ask for. He talked of nothing else! I'm not sure if the Special Wish Foundation bent their rules, or if they granted him one wish, and other people who had heard that he had three wishes found a way to make the other two happen, but in the end he got all three of his wishes.

I spent hours with Tommy and his mom. Tommy eventually trusted me enough to let his mom leave the room if I would stay with him. For the first time in months, she was able to take a long shower, eat a nonhospital meal, or spend time with her fiancé. I would try to ask Tommy about his illness, but he would always change the subject or tell me firmly that he didn't want to talk about that. He wanted to play, so we played.

I worried that this didn't seem very chaplain-like, and I was afraid I wasn't helping him face his death peacefully. I met with my supervisor, Toni, and told her that I felt concerned about Tommy because he never spoke about his illness or death. I was worried that maybe he didn't understand how sick he was, and that perhaps he should know in case there was something he needed to do or say before he died. I also wondered why he never mentioned God and was concerned he would be afraid when he died because he didn't know God yet. Toni encouraged me to stop worrying and just be with him.

He became sicker and sicker, and it became more and more certain he was not going to win his battle against cancer. No one told Tommy, nor did we discuss it in front of him. His mother was afraid it would scare him, so we respected her request and said nothing. Also, he was four, and we weren't sure he could comprehend what death was.

Eventually I got a call from Tommy's nurses, who said he had asked to speak to me. He was very sick by then. He had sores in his mouth and didn't want to eat. He was extremely thin and rarely sat up anymore. He still played, but he lay down as he did so.

I went into his room, and he said, "Leanne, I don't know if you know this, but I'm very sick. I might die."

I said nothing.

"I know I've had my three special wishes, but I have one more thing I've never done, and I'd like to do it. Do you think you could help me?"

I was in tears and prepared to do anything in my power to make this child's dying wish a reality. "What do you want, honey?" I asked.

"Can you get a little closer so I can whisper it? I'm very tired," he said.

I moved closer and placed my ear by his little mouth, listening as closely as I could. "What is it? You can ask me anything!" I said.

He spoke softly but clearly, saying, "I've never had a beer and lobster dinner. Do you think I could have it?"

I couldn't help but laugh and wasn't sure if we could make this wish happen or not. I promised to ask his doctor and see what he said. My plan was to say no and blame it on "doctor's orders." To my astonishment, his doctor liked the idea. He would bring the beer if I would buy the lobster.

The next night we all gathered in Tommy's room—me, the doctor, Tommy's mother, her fiancé, and of course Tommy. He loved the lobster and dipped each bite into the melted butter. I'm not sure what he ate more of—the butter or the lobster. But he didn't like the beer. He took one taste, spit it out, and went back to eating his lobster. That was the last night I remember him sitting up and laughing.

One day I went into his room to check on him. I asked his mother if she wanted to go out and grab a Coke since I had time to sit with him. I promised to call her if he should get worse or needed her.

"Why don't you both go get a Coke together!" Tommy said.

He had never suggested this, and we were both shocked.

"Whenever you're alone, you get into trouble," I reminded him, "so I need to stay with you while your mommy goes out."

"No, you should go together," he insisted.

"Why?" I asked.

"Because *she* is here," he said. "Isn't she beautiful?"

His mother and I looked around the room, but there was no one there except the three of us. "Where is she?" his mother asked.

He seemed a bit irritated at her silly question and pointed to the edge of his bed. "She's there. I need to talk to her alone, so you two need to go get a Coke together."

We left the room, and for the first time in months, Tommy was alone. We fully expected a call from the nurses' station, telling us to come back, but the call never came. When we returned to his room he was asleep, the sheets still on the bed, no sign of distress, and all his monitors still connected.

As time went on, he spoke often of "her." He would ask us to leave so they could talk, and he would often speak to her as if she was one of the people in the room. He would look over at what seemed to be an empty spot and simply nod his head or smile as if he'd heard something wonderful. He told us where she was and never described her as anything except beautiful. And with the way he said the word, we all knew that she was something extraordinary. She wasn't beautiful like a woman would be, but like a baby bird learning to fly or a child seeing their first rainbow. He never seemed to grow tired of her presence or to stop being fascinated by her beauty. Each time he described her as beautiful, it was as if he was seeing her for the first time.

He started asking questions about his death. He wanted to know if it would hurt. He wanted to know if his dog, which had died years earlier, would be in heaven. He wanted to know if little children missed their mommies in heaven. He would ask these questions, not really wanting us to say anything, but staring at the spot where "she" was.

One night as I was leaving his room, he asked me a question. "Leanne, would Mommy be mad at me if I went with 'her'? I want to go with her now. I'm tired."

I began to cry. I wanted to tell him to stay with us and not to go with her because we would miss him. But I said what I knew was correct. "No," I said, "your mommy won't be angry. It's okay."

His mother, who was sitting in her chair next to his bed, said nothing. She simply leaned over and kissed him. It is amazing to me that a kiss can say more than words ever could. He went to sleep, and I sat by his bed for a long time.

A few nights later, I was home in bed and my pager went off. I knew it was Tommy before I even called the hospital. I threw on my shoes and drove there as fast as I could. Everyone was standing in a line, looking exhausted and sort of leaning for support on the walls in the hallway. I asked what was going on. They explained that Tommy's body was slowing down. He had an irregular heartbeat and his breathing was labored. When I asked why they were in the hallway, they said he had requested them to leave so he could be alone with "her." A few moments later, his nurse went in to check on him, and he had died.

A quiet fell over all of us. It was so quiet you could almost hear the silence. We stood there, no one saying a word. His mother was the first to speak, and she said, "I'm so happy that she was with him."

In that holy, quiet moment, even a student chaplain knew to stay silent.

3

Shane

Shane was one of the first children I met at the hospital. His record indicated that this was his third admit to the hospital, so I decided I would visit him and introduce myself.

Introducing myself was something I dreaded. I was young, and while I felt like a grown-up, I look back at my pictures now and see I was, in reality, a typical twenty-two-year-old girl trying to look professional. Often when I would walk into a room and tell people I was the chaplain, I would get one of two responses. They would ask, "Are you here because my child is dying?" or "How old are you?"

The first question was easy to answer. I would explain that chaplains visited each child and family upon admittance just to let them know we were available in case they needed us. We did more than just visit when a child was dying; we would be good listeners, because all visits to the hospital with a child are stressful.

The second question, about my age, was more difficult to answer because, to be honest, it hurt my feelings and embarrassed me. I had tried my best to dress professionally and look older than I was, and this question reminded me that I was young and not fooling anyone. It also made me doubt whether I had the skills needed to be a chaplain to these children and their parents. But not sure of what else to do, I would reluctantly tell them my age and then assure them that while I was young, I was well trained and supervised. I would smile and pretend that I wasn't bothered one little bit by their question.

I remember my first visit with Shane vividly. He was sitting up eating his breakfast, and his mother was sitting in a chair next to his bed. There were all kinds of signs in his room reminding us to wash our hands thoroughly and put on a gown. I began washing my hands and introduced myself over the sound of running water, then put on a gown and walked over to the bed.

Shane's mother smiled and said, "You're the chaplain? Well, thank you for visiting us." I might recall this visit to Shane so well because it was the first time I wasn't asked one of the two dreaded questions!

Shane was a beautiful child. He had thick black hair, deep brown eyes, and sort of a stocky build. He wasn't heavy but rather looked like a kid who would be great on a football field. I knew from his many admits that he must be quite sick, but he didn't look like it.

I noticed a bag of blood hanging on an IV pole beside his bed. He must have seen me looking at it, because he said, "That's blood, you know. I had to come in because my platelet count got low again."

Shane had recently been diagnosed with a disease called aplastic anemia, a rare blood disease where the body, for some unknown reason, stops producing enough red blood cells. Shane's blood count had to be monitored closely, and whenever it became too low, he had to come to the hospital and get some new blood cells. His mother told me they called the red blood cells "energy cells," because when they were low he would be extremely tired and lethargic, but after receiving new blood cells he would be bouncing off the walls! She and Shane told me about how nutty he would act after getting a blood transfusion.

I learned all about a disease I had never heard of. No one mentioned that it was life threatening, but I could tell it was a serious disease by the look in Shane's mother's eyes. She was smiling, telling stories, making fun of Shane, and laughing, but there was sadness in those eyes. I knew without being told that she was frightened and worried.

Shane had five younger sisters who were stair steps in age from about two years to eight. Shane was ten. Visits from his sisters were always dependent on his blood counts. If the blood count was above a certain number, the kids could visit their brother. If it was below a certain number, they could not. Shane never complained about getting his blood count taken, because that was the only way he would know if his sisters, whom he adored, could visit.

He was the most loving and sweetest older brother I think I've ever known. Sometimes older brothers find their younger sisters to be pests or annoying, or they pick on their sisters and delight in making them scream. But watching Shane with his sisters was more like watching a father play with his children. He would patiently read stories to them, asking on each page of the book where the ball was or what color the boots were. He would help them do their puzzles just like an attuned and loving parent or teacher might, but he wouldn't do the work for them. I was struck by the maturity, patience, and understanding he had for these little ones.

And his sisters adored him! I loved to watch them walking down the hospital hallway. They had been instructed not to run, so no one did, but they walked as fast as they could, and their smiles would get larger and their giggles louder with every step toward his room. Then they would push and wiggle past each other, trying to be the first one in the room so they could scrub up, put on a gown, and receive the first hug. Shane wouldn't get out of bed but sat there waiting for each little sister to climb up and hug him. After they were all on the bed, he looked like a Native American storytelling doll—the ones I find in gift shops, made of clay, where a person is sitting down and children are covering almost every part of their body.

I loved visiting Shane and his family. They were the most genuine and loving family I had ever met. His was seriously ill, yet whenever the family was there, the room was filled with joy and happiness. To see and hear this family interact, you never would have known that he was sick!

We all knew, though, that Shane was a very sick child. There was no certain cure for aplastic anemia, and blood transfusions became less effective as time went on. Shane needed to come into the hospital more and more often. He was also beginning to look sick. His skin was pale, almost clear. He had developed dark circles under his eyes. I don't know if the dark circles had worsened or had simply become more apparent because he was so pale. He was more and more lethargic, and even after receiving blood, he would no longer bounce off the walls, as he and his mother had laughed about at our first visit. Now he would talk and laugh after the transfusions, but he stayed in bed and slept most of the time. Instead of coming in to the hospital periodically, he would spend most of his time in the hospital and go home periodically.

One of the things that bothered Shane the most about getting worse was that because his blood counts weren't coming up as they once had, his sisters weren't able to visit as often. When he did feel well, he would draw pictures and make cards for them, telling them how much he missed them and loved them. Sometimes, when it had been a long time between visits, they would come to the hospital and look at him through the window of his room. He would make funny faces and show them the pictures he had drawn for them, and they would dissolve into giggles. Even when he felt at his worst, when his sisters would visit he was happy.

After about a year, the cancer doctors started talking to his parents about a treatment that was still in the experimental phase but that they hoped would cure him of his disease. It was a bone marrow transplant. They explained it was a very difficult treatment and would be rough on Shane's body. Red blood cells are made in the bone marrow, and with aplastic anemia patients, the bone marrow stops making them. In this procedure, Shane's existing bone marrow would need to be completely killed and new bone marrow transplanted, in the hope that the new marrow would begin working properly. It was a risky procedure because if it didn't work, he would die. On the other hand, he was already dying. Shane's only hope for survival was a successful transplant.

Shane had known he was very sick. His parents and the doctors had been open and honest with him along each step of his illness. They told him about the transplant and asked him if it was something he would agree to. I was there when they talked to him and was struck by the respect and sensitivity that his parents always had toward him. It was no wonder he showed the same respect and care toward his little sisters.

He asked a few questions and looked carefully at the diagrams they had drawn for him. He had only one question regarding the isolation bed. Because one of the tasks of red blood cells is to help with a person's immune system, killing all of the bone marrow would mean that Shane's immunity would be zero. He would not be allowed to come into contact with any germs for several weeks, before and following the bone marrow transplant.

Shane would be placed in a bed that was completely enclosed by a huge plastic square, with a zipper that would open on one end. He would crawl in, and then he could be touched only by the doctors and nurses, as well as items such as his food tray that had been carefully prepared or games and toys that had been thoroughly sterilized. People could see him and talk to him, though the sound would be muffled because of the plastic. None of his family or friends would be able to touch him directly, but there were gloves attached to the bed. His mother and father could place their hands through holes and into the gloves and touch him. However, there would be plastic separating them, and there would be no skin-to-skin contact for many weeks.

Shane listened carefully, nodding and asking clarifying questions. And then for the first time in his entire illness, he started to cry. He didn't wail or sob, he simply cried. Tears ran down his face. His mother moved to his bed and held him. And then in the tiniest whisper, he said, "No hugs and kisses from my sisters for a month? They'll miss me so much!" He was worried not about himself but about them.

It took several days to get everything ready. Releases needed to be signed, every one of Shane's vital organs needed to be tested, and more education about the transplant had to be given to his parents. During this time, Shane was receiving blood nearly every day. If there had been any doubt before about this transplant being his only chance of survival, there was none now. Everyone was in agreement it needed to happen. Our hospital was not equipped to do bone marrow transplants, so he was moved to a larger hospital a few miles away.

Shane's sisters hadn't been able to visit very often for fear they would expose him to a germ or illness, but special arrangements were made for a party the night before the transplant procedure was to begin. Everyone was there in the hospital room. We had cake, ice cream, and pop, and there was, as usual, laughing and hugging and joy. But there was also a certain heaviness. I had never seen such intense sadness and fear in Shane's mother's eyes.

Shane tried to act like the transplant was no big deal and he was ready, but I could hear that he was scared by the tone of his voice, and his bottom lip would shake just the tiniest bit when he would assure us that he was fine.

Throughout the party, his five little sisters never moved from his side, and never, even when he ate his cake, did he stop touching one or another of them. While touching was not encouraged, the girls had scrubbed their hands as carefully as possible, and they wore gowns that were made for adults and dragged on the floor as they walked. I thought maybe a nurse or doctor would ask Shane not to touch his sisters, but no one did. In reality, I'm not sure anyone could have prevented that even if they had tried.

I had never seen a bone marrow transplant. The procedure was much more difficult and demanding on Shane's body than

I imagined. I had worried about how an active ten-year-old would be able to tolerate being cooped up in a plastic bed for a month, but during and after the procedure I understood. He was so sick and so weak that he slept most of the time. It was rare to visit and find him awake.

His parents took turns sitting with him and never left his side. Shane mostly woke up to eat, though he wasn't eating often or well. When he did wake up, the first question he asked, without fail, was, "How are my sisters?" And before falling back to sleep, he would tell his parents, "Let them know how much I miss them and love them."

Shane's transplant didn't work. He began to run extremely high fevers. Infection had set in. We all knew that it was only a matter of days before he would die.

On one of those last days, his mother called me to visit. Shane was asking for me. I got to the hospital as fast as I could and saw him awake and smiling. I hadn't seen him awake or smiling for several weeks. In fact, I hadn't seen him this alert since the procedure began.

He wanted to show me a picture he had drawn of a dream he had during the night. The picture was of his five sisters. They were happy, holding hands, and playing a game together. Above them floated a set of clouds, and above the clouds was Shane with angel wings. He was standing beside a person made of light, who he told me was God. They were both smiling and watching over the children below.

"Leanne," Shane said, "I've been really afraid of dying because I've always known that my job on earth was to be a big brother to my sisters. It was my job to take care of them and show them things and teach them things. I didn't want to die because I'm the only big brother they have and I needed to be here. But tonight God told me that when I die, he'll let me watch over them and take care of them. I'll still get to do my job! I'll still be their big brother! So I drew them this picture so they'll never forget their big brother still loves them and is taking care of them."

Shane died a few days after he showed me his picture. I wasn't there, but his parents told me his death was peaceful. He had gone to sleep and slipped away without a sound.

Shane's funeral was a beautiful service, but I must admit I heard very little of what was said. I could not take my eyes off the pew where his family was seated. His mother sat on one end and his father on the other, with his five little sisters between them. They were sad and so still. I had never seen his sisters sit still before, and my heart was breaking for them.

After the service I hugged Shane's parents and the girls. I reached out to take hold of his mother's hand and realized she was holding something that was folded tightly. She smiled through her tears and handed it to me. I carefully unfolded it and realized it was the picture Shane had drawn. I folded it back up and placed it back into her hand. We hugged again and we both cried.

I hugged each of Shane's little sisters and could not help but wonder if they would ever understand how deeply they were loved by their big brother. I suppose it really didn't matter. Whether they knew it or not, these little girls had a brother who would watch over, protect, and guide them for the rest of their lives. God had told him so!

4

Rebecca

In all my years working with children, I have observed that while children are each unique and wonderfully individual, they still tend to fall into two categories: those who are serious most of the time and those who are silly most of the time. It is nearly impossible to make a serious child act silly or to make a silly child be serious. Rebecca was one of those children who loved being silly. She giggled all the time, and she paid no attention to anything that she didn't consider funny.

I met Rebecca the first day she was admitted to the hospital. It was late in the afternoon, nearly time for me to leave for the day, but I decided to make one final call before I left. I had been notified that a little girl, nine years old, had been admitted because she'd been diagnosed with leukemia. I expected to enter a somber room, but when I got there, I saw a little girl with long, wavy, bright red hair down to her waist, standing in front of who I assumed were her parents and her nurse and singing a song from the musical *Annie*. They smiled and clapped loudly as she finished the song, dramatically raised her arms over her head, and took a deep bow.

I entered the room and introduced myself, and during the next five minutes I learned Rebecca had three kittens and that she wanted to be a singer when she grew up. Her parents were warm and friendly. They shared that she had been feeling tired, which I could clearly see was not normal for her, so they had taken her to the doctor. Tests had been run, and they had revealed she had leukemia.

There are different kinds of leukemia. Rebecca's parents told me she had the type that wasn't easily treatable, but the doctor was hopeful the treatments could contain it and at least get her into remission, which, once achieved, could last for years. They were hoping the cancer would not return at all. She would begin chemo the next day.

During the entire time I was listening to her parents, Rebecca was busy organizing her room. Many people had already sent her flowers and balloon bouquets, and she was humming and moving them from place to place, trying to figure out exactly where each one should be placed to make her room pretty. She appeared not to listen to us, but if you know children at all, you know they are always listening.

"Do you have any questions about the chemotherapy?" I asked Rebecca. "Because if you do, I can get a nurse to answer them."

"No!" she said. "I'm not thinking about it and I don't want to talk about it!" Her game plan was clear: she was going to ignore the whole thing until it went away!

Lots of children do this. I call it "wishful peekaboo." Children of all ages, when they don't want to do something or face something, pretend not to hear you or notice it. In doing so, they're wishing that whatever is facing them will disappear.

This was Rebecca's plan. She would not talk about cancer, learn about it, or acknowledge it in any way, and it would go away.

Unfortunately, the next morning the cancer was still there. I stopped by Rebecca's room, and she was sitting in the reclining chair next to her bed, with an IV in her arm and a bag of the chemo drip above her. She was dressed in pajamas that looked like a clown suit. They were bright red and matched her long hair. The collar was white and ruffled, there were three huge pom-poms on the front for buttons, and the ruffled cuffs covered her hands and feet. Her hair was divided into five ponytails. One was on the very top of her head, two stuck out the sides, and two came out the back. She was the most adorable little clown I've ever seen.

I came in and asked Rebecca how she felt. "I'm great!" she replied, but I could tell she was having a hard time holding her coloring book in the proper position because she had only one hand free. The other hand was taped to the board of the chair to steady it while she received her chemotherapy.

She chattered and giggled. "Oh, I love this lion picture! Did I ever tell you that I went to the circus once? I did, and I loved it, except this one part."

"Were you scared of something that happened during the show?" I asked.

"Oh no, I'm not scared of anything! I loved it. But anyway, I was eating a huge ice cream cone—one dip chocolate, one dip strawberry. It started to melt, so I took a big lick, and it came right out of the cone and fell—*plop*—onto the woman in front of me!" She dissolved into giggles. I laughed too. Her giggles were contagious.

When Rebecca finished coloring her lion, she began coloring a picture of a kitten. "My kitten looks sort of like this one, only mine has stripes. When I first got him, I slept with him in my bed. Then this one morning I woke up and he was gone. I mean, we looked all over the house and couldn't find him anywhere!"

"That must have been so scary!" I said.

"It was, but the weird thing was that I could hear his little meow. I followed the sound, and you'll never guess where he was." Before I had a chance to answer, she exclaimed, "He had fallen between the sheet and bed, where the sheets get tucked in. Poor old thing—there he was stuck in the bed like a little caterpillar in a cocoon!" Once more the two of us dissolved into laughter. If there hadn't been an IV in her arm, I never would have known that she was starting a long battle with cancer.

Each time I visited Rebecca, she was still laughing and had her clown pajamas on. I soon realized she refused to wear anything else. And each time her hair was done up in some fun style. Ponytails one day, a bun on her head with pencils poked through it to hold it in place another day, and braids of all shapes and sizes on yet another day. She loved silly hairdos and all the laughter and attention they brought her.

Rebecca finished her first course of treatment and went home. A few weeks later she returned to the hospital for a second round of treatment, and she still wore her clown pajamas every day. She was still fixing her hair in crazy styles, but there was clearly less of it, and more bald spaces appeared between each ponytail or braid. Before long her hair was falling out in clumps, and because it was so long, it was wrapping all around her arms and legs and was simply a mess. The staff approached her mother and asked if they could shave Rebecca's head. Her mother agreed to the request but was in tears.

I hadn't arrived to work yet when they shaved all that long, beautiful, wavy red hair off, so when I did arrive I immediately ran to Rebecca's room. She was sitting in the large chair with her back to the door. I knocked and went in. She didn't say a word.

"Rebecca, I heard your hair got shaved off today. You okay?" I asked.

Again, she didn't say a word.

"I brought you a new coloring book about kittens," I said. "You want to color?"

Yet again, she didn't say anything.

I knew she must feel upset and embarrassed not to have her hair anymore, and I didn't want to further embarrass her by looking at her if she didn't want me to, so I asked, "Do you want me to see you now that your hair is gone, or do you want me to just leave the coloring book here by the sink and come back later?"

All of a sudden she popped up over the back of the chair like a jack-in-the-box, and she had a bright red clown nose on her face. "I surprised you, huh?" she said, and we laughed and laughed. She had been sitting there all that time just waiting for the right moment to surprise me!

I asked her how she felt without hair, but she refused to acknowledge my question and started coloring with me and telling me all her funny stories. Her plan was still in place. She would not think or talk about anything that was happening to her, and it would go away.

Over the course of the next year, Rebecca would come and go from the hospital. Her first course of treatment didn't work, nor did the second. The hospital staff started watching her blood counts closely. When they dropped, her risk of infection would be high, and since leukemia affects the blood cells, her blood wouldn't be able to fight off infection.

Rebecca would come into the hospital every time her blood counts dropped below a certain number. She had to spend much time in isolation. The staff brought her things to play with and tried to keep her occupied, but despite their efforts, her laughter and silliness started to turn to anger. She didn't like the hospital food, complained of being bored, was sick of coloring and doing puzzles, and wanted to go home. Her parents brought her food from home and her favorite restaurants, but she still complained that it wasn't what she wanted to eat. They brought her new toys and things to play with, but she still complained of being bored. I would visit her, but she no longer wanted to tell me her funny stories. She wanted to be left alone.

She was an angry little girl. No one could blame her. Her plan of wishful peekaboo was not working. Early on she had decided to ignore the leukemia, and it would go away. Yet she had done all in her power to ignore it, and it was still there. She had colored the entire time she received her chemo, sung songs during the painful tests, and laughed when they shaved her head. She had refused to acknowledge it, and it was still there!

The doctors told Rebecca and her parents that they could not do any further treatments until her body became stronger again. They would continue giving her blood to keep infection out. The plan was to give her body a rest and hopefully try treatment again later. As much as they didn't want to, the doctors also told Rebecca and her parents that there was a possibility she might die.

You would think the news that she might die would have driven Rebecca further into depression and anger, but it actually had the opposite effect. She became more animated and talkative than ever before. Now, more than ever, she was going to ignore the cancer and make it go away! It was nice to see her smile and to spend time with her again.

Her hair had started to grow back in. It was barely over two inches long, and she used tiny rubber bands to make ponytails along the top of her head, where her bangs would eventually be. Once she figured out that rubber bands could go back in her hair, she also figured out that she could stick other things in the rubber bands. One day when I visited, she had a different-colored feather sticking out of each rubber band. She looked like a peacock! Another day she had plastic spoons sticking out of the rubber bands. We laughed and laughed at her silly hair.

Her parents asked me if I would mind talking to her about dying. They weren't religious people. They had both grown up in the church but had stopped attending during college and had not returned. They sort of believed in God, but they had never really taught Rebecca anything about him and hadn't taken her to church. They were worried that she might be scared but had no idea how to bring up the subject of dying to her. She was a master at not talking about anything she didn't want to, so I doubted if I could get her to talk, but I told her parents I would try.

Once when Rebecca and I were alone, I sat on the side of her bed coloring with her. She was coloring a picture of a rainbow and a pot of gold. She was telling me she believed in leprechauns because she had seen one once and nearly found the pot of gold. But her cat was with her and probably scared the leprechaun away before she could catch him.

When she finished her story, I told her that I thought leprechauns could also grant wishes. "If you had a wish, what would it be?" I asked her.

She giggled and replied, "To catch a leprechaun and get the gold!"

I laughed and then asked again, "Seriously, what is your deepest wish?"

She was quiet, looked me directly in the eyes, and said, "I wish that I don't die."

"Are you afraid?" I asked.

Her eyes got big and she looked at me like I was crazy. "Afraid?" she said, as if I were asking the most ridiculous question in the world. "No, I'm not afraid at all! I'll go to heaven, but I don't want to. I know what they do in heaven. They sing quiet songs and whisper all the time. It'll be boring, and I don't want to go there! It'll be worse than this stupid, boring hospital!" Her eyes flashed with anger, and she closed the coloring book and started putting the crayons away. It was clear that she was finished with the conversation.

Suddenly she got a huge smile on her face and said, "You know what we should do, Leanne? We should have a slumber party! You can bring your pajamas, and we can fix each other's hair and eat pizza and stay up all night. Will you have a slumber party with me? It'll be so much fun! Come on, let's have a sleepover!"

I told her I wasn't sure if I could, but I would ask her parents and my boss. I hated to tell her no, but I really didn't want to stay up all night, and though she thought it would be the most fun thing in the world, I didn't think it sounded fun at all.

From that day on, every time I visited her, she would ask me if I had checked about the slumber party and when it was going to happen. I asked my boss, who said she didn't see why I couldn't do it as long as her mother was there. Rebecca asked her mom if we could have a slumber party, and she said she would order the pizzas for us.

Everyone except me thought this was a great idea. I loved Rebecca, but the idea of losing sleep when I was already tired from school and work was just not what I wanted. Then I asked the staff their opinion, hoping they would think it was a bad idea because of germs or something. They thought it was adorable that she wanted to have a sleepover. They offered to bring a third bed into the room so I could at least lie down. We all knew I wouldn't sleep!

I avoided the sleepover as long as I could. Lots of Fridays I already had legitimate plans. On others I made up excuses. Every time I left her room, though, Rebecca reminded me to find a date because the sleepover was going to be great!

After a few months, it became more obvious that Rebecca was losing the battle against cancer. Her blood counts were bad even after blood was given, and she began to develop tiny red spots that resembled bruising under her skin. I knew this was a sign that her body was breaking down. The doctors confirmed that she was getting weaker, and the hope of doing further treatments was slipping away. She was tired and not as animated as before, but she continued to smile and still invited me to have a slumber party.

She had been a trouper through this illness. The least I could do was miss a night's sleep and have a party with this sweet little girl.

On the Friday of the party, a third bed was brought into her room, and the pizza arrived right on schedule. Rebecca was happy and had more energy than she'd had in days. We spent the evening eating, painting our fingernails and toenails, putting makeup on, and fixing our hair. We did all the things little girls do at slumber parties.

Rebecca was clearly in full control of the entire evening. She had strong opinions about how our makeup should look and thought I put on far less blush and eye shadow than I needed. She put blue eye shadow on both of us, plus lots of blush and deep red lipstick. We both had several ponytails sticking out from our heads in every direction. We were—at least in Rebecca's opinion—beautiful!

I had a better time at our party than I'd ever dreamed. It had been a long time since I'd let myself be silly and have fun. And with Rebecca in charge of the party, we had fun.

As the night wore on, Rebecca's mother went to sleep. Rebecca and I tried to, but we got the giggles. Every time we got quiet, one of us would start to laugh. This went on and on. You know, once you start laughing, it's almost impossible to stop.

Finally we did stop and the room was quiet. We had been so loud and laughed so much that the silence was almost audible.

I was sitting on my bed facing Rebecca, who was lying in her bed. She whispered, "Leanne, remember how I told you my wish, how I told you I didn't want to die? Remember how I told you heaven would be boring? It isn't!"

"What?" I whispered back to her, not sure what else to say.

"Heaven. Do you know about heaven? You know, where you go after you die?" she said, making sure I knew the basic facts.

"Yes, I know about heaven. I'm just unsure about what you're talking about."

She began whispering louder now, clearly growing frustrated with my lack of understanding. "I'm talking about heaven. I thought it was boring, but it isn't. They told me . . . you know . . . the people, but you know they aren't really people . . . but they tell you and show you heaven. And they showed me, and it isn't boring. It's beautiful, and you can laugh there and have fun, and there are kittens . . . oh, and the rainbows are so pretty. I just wanted to tell you it isn't boring at all there. I'll laugh when I get there and play with kittens and climb on the rainbows if I want to. And time goes very fast there, so I won't miss my kittens or Mom and Dad at all, because after I play for just a little while, they'll be there with me. I just wanted you to know."

I pressed her to tell me more details. I wanted to know who exactly told her these things. I wanted to know what these "people" looked like and exactly what they said and what they told her. She listened to my questions and then said, "I don't want to talk about it. I just wanted you to know." And then she fell asleep.

I thought I would be up all night because of Rebecca, but it was the beauty of the vision of heaven she had shared with me that kept me awake while she peacefully slept.

Rebecca died a few months after our slumber party. Now I never see a rainbow that doesn't make me think of her. I can almost hear her laughter as I imagine her playing with kittens, telling her funny stories, and never being bored!

5

James

James was ten years old and had been admitted to the hospital because of a benign brain tumor. I walked to his room to introduce myself, but before I knocked, I could see through the window that I needed to wait before I entered. The family was deep in prayer.

While I waited, I peeked into the room. James was not in a hospital gown as most kids were but rather had on creased blue slacks and a button-down white shirt neatly tucked in. He had on black dress shoes and a black belt. His hair was conservatively cut, parted on the side, and stayed in place because of some kind of hair gel. He looked like a little man instead of a boy.

His father, who was dressed exactly like James, was sitting in a chair by the window, and his mother was sitting next to James on his bed. They were doing their morning devotions. I later learned they did this faithfully every day as a family. They would read from the Bible, say the Lord's Prayer, and then sit in silence until they felt moved by the Holy Spirit to pray. One at a time, they would each say a prayer. Then they would join hands and ask God's blessing to be upon them, their family, their friends, and all who needed it. After James's diagnosis, they added the doctors, nurses, and hospital staff to the list of blessings.

When they finished their prayers, I knocked and entered the room. I introduced myself to them, and they told me their names and thanked me for coming. James's father stood up and asked me if I wanted to sit down. James stuck out his hand and shook mine as warmly and confidently as any adult would.

I spent a few minutes getting to know them and then excused myself to visit other patients. Before I left, James's father asked, "Would you pray for us?"

I suddenly felt insecure. I could tell from watching this family pray together earlier that they were already prayer warriors! These people knew how to pray; what could I possibly add?

"What would you like me to pray for?" I asked

"For complete healing of our son's tumor," they said.

We held hands, and I asked God to work with the medical staff and to heal James completely. As I prayed, James and his mother and father whispered their agreement with, "Yes, Lord" and "Jesus, we trust you." I could feel the presence and power of God in the room, not because of the words I prayed but because these people had truly authentic faith. They believed with all their heart and soul that Jesus would answer their prayer. I wasn't sure how God's healing worked exactly, but if it happened because of sincere prayers, then James was certainly going to be healed.

When James's family and friends heard his tumor was noncancerous, they were relieved. However, whenever a tumor is located in the brain or on the spine, even when it's not cancerous, it's dangerous and can be life threatening. When a tumor is located in a muscle, the tumor and the tissue around it are removed to make sure it won't grow back. Since the brain is filled with blood vessels, nerves, and neurons, it is difficult to remove a tumor without disturbing the function of the brain. Doctors face a difficult task to remove a tumor without disturbing the tissue around it. Sometimes the tumor cannot be completely removed because the damage to the brain would be too great. And sometimes doctors think they have removed all of it and later discover a tiny amount of tumor cells remaining, and the tumor grows back.

James and his family, while relieved that they were not facing a battle with cancer, knew that they still had a serious illness to deal with. They would say their devotions every morning, and before any test or radiation treatment, they would join hands and pray for God to be with the medical staff and to heal James completely. Many times their minister would join them, and I tell you, that man could pray! Every time he finished, I felt like I'd been to an old-fashioned tent revival. These people and their deep faith inspired me and challenged me to think about what I believed about the power of prayer and the miracle of healing.

The radiation treatments went well. James never complained. He dressed in street clothes every day and only put on the hospital gown for sleeping and when he needed treatments. He lay perfectly still during his treatments and even said "thank you" every time he finished radiation or when he had blood drawn.

Visiting James was like visiting an adult. He knew his Bible as well as any adult I had ever met. He thought a lot about God. You might assume he was thinking about God's ability to heal or about something related to his illness. But he pondered God's will for him. He wanted to follow God and do the things God required of him, such as love his enemies and care for those who had less than he did. One of his favorite Bible passages was the one where Jesus talks about the sheep and the goats and tells of a day when we will all be judged. James wanted to enter the gate of the sheep. He wanted Jesus to be proud of him because he had fed the poor, visited the sick, and clothed the naked.

I had never met a child before who was so focused on following Jesus. And he was so sincere about it. He wasn't simply repeating what he had heard in church; he was reading the Bible, praying, and choosing a life of following God.

James was also very interested in the other children in the hospital. He wanted to pray for them to be healed. Each time I visited him, we prayed together, holding hands and waiting for the Holy Spirit. I would pray, and then he would pray. I was struck by the fact that he never prayed for himself, and one day I asked him why. He told me that he could not find a place in the Bible where God asked us to care for ourselves. "God cares for us," he told me, "so we don't have to. And since he cares for us, we can care for others and not worry about ourselves."

The radiation treatments went well, and the size of the tumor was greatly reduced. Everyone was hopeful that James would have a positive outcome after surgery.

The staff began explaining the surgery to the family. There were many risks. The surgeons would certainly try to avoid removing any part of James's brain that could affect his movement or speech, but there were no guarantees.

Early the next morning while I was still at home, my pager went off. I called the hospital, and the operator told me that James's nurse needed me to come in right away. I dressed as quickly as I could, arrived at the hospital, and went straight to the nurses' station.

James's nurse was upset. She explained to me that she had gone in to visit James when her shift had started, and he had started talking and showed a bad attitude about his surgery. She didn't want him to go into such a serious surgery with a poor attitude. She asked me to talk to him.

I went into his room, expecting to see an upset or angry child. But James was sitting up and smiled as I walked into the room. We talked for a few minutes, and there was nothing abnormal about him. He wasn't upset, he wasn't angry, and he wasn't depressed. I asked him how he felt about the surgery, and he said fine. I asked if he was upset because they would have to shave off even more of his hair, and he wasn't. I saw no sign of a bad attitude.

Finally I told him that I had been called in because his nurse was worried that he had a negative attitude about the surgery. He had no idea what I was talking about. I decided I needed to ask his nurse what he had said that made her so upset.

As I was leaving the room, James said, "Leanne, I need to ask you something."

"Yes?" I replied.

"Is there time for me to be baptized before my surgery?"

"I think so," I said. "But why? Is there any special reason you want to be baptized?"

"Because God told me to in my dream," he replied nonchalantly.

It began to dawn on me that this dream might have been what he had shared with the nurse. "Did you have a dream last night?" I asked.

"Yes, I did," James said. "I dreamed that I was in a field. It was very large and had green grass. I was by myself, but I wasn't afraid. I was waiting, but I didn't know who I was waiting for. I knew they would come, though. And then a bridge appeared in front of me. It was white and made out of wood. It was one of those arching bridges, like the one in the story *Three Billy Goats Gruff*.

"At first I couldn't see Jesus. I only saw his light. It was on the other side of the bridge and moving toward me. Before it got to the bridge, the light began to turn into Jesus. I knew him immediately. He didn't have to tell me who he was—I knew! He was beautiful. Everything was beautiful! He was dressed in a white gown. It was made of light—well, sort of material, but light. I can't explain it.

"He started to cross the bridge, and I started to run toward him. We met at the top of the curved part of the bridge and hugged. His hug was as warm a feeling as the light was bright. We hugged for a long time, and he kept telling me how proud he was of me because I read my Bible and say my prayers and love other people. I knew he was proud because of his words, but I could also *feel* he was proud by his hug.

"Jesus asked me if I wanted to cross the bridge with him. I did! I wanted to go wherever he went! So he took my hand and we crossed the bridge, and he showed me heaven. Leanne, heaven is so beautiful. It isn't what you expect, because we have never seen anything as beautiful as it is. I wish I could tell you what it looked like, but I can't. It was more beautiful than anything I've ever seen, and it had things in it that I've never seen before, but I belonged there. We all belong there.

"I don't know how long I stayed in heaven, but Jesus told me it was time to go home. Then he told me that he showed me heaven because I would be coming here in three months and he didn't want me to worry or be afraid. He said my surgery will go fine, but I'll still die in three months. He promised to meet me on the bridge again, hold my hand, and stay with me for eternity.

"Then I was back on the other side of the bridge, and all I could see was his light. I turned to go home, and he told me that I needed to be baptized before surgery. So can I be baptized?"

I was speechless. I sat there in the hospital with this child in the holiness of the moment. His description of heaven was so wonderful I had nothing to say.

My silence was interrupted by James saying again, "Leanne, can I be baptized?"

"Yes, of course," I said, coming back to reality. "I mean, we have to ask your parents, but I can't imagine they won't agree."

I went back to the nurse and told her that James wanted to be baptized before surgery. We only had a few hours until he would be taken to the operating room.

She didn't want him to be baptized. "He's preparing to die, and he needs to have a positive attitude for surgery," she said.

"He has no fear of dying in surgery," I reminded her. In fact, he had been told that the surgery would go well.

The nurse reluctantly called his parents, who had just arrived at the hospital. They, of course, agreed that if James wanted to be baptized, he should be. They tried to contact their pastor, but he didn't answer his phone. It was still quite early, and I assumed he was asleep.

James's parents asked if I would baptize James if their pastor couldn't be located. I wasn't yet ordained, so technically

I wasn't allowed to baptize, but in the case of an emergency I could. This constituted an emergency in my mind, so I agreed. I went to my office and found a pretty glass bowl to place the water in. I filled it and said a prayer over it and then carried it to James's room. I placed the bowl on his hospital tray and explained that I had blessed the water and would use it to baptize him.

He took one look at the water and started to laugh. Then his mother and father started to laugh with him. I was confused. James looked at me and said, "You're going to use that? We're Baptist—I need to be dunked under the water!" I joined them in their laughter and tried to think of a Plan B.

I took my problem back to the nurses' station, and much to my surprise, the nurse who had opposed the baptism suggested we use one of the whirlpools. The water would be cool if we didn't turn the motors on. So we readied the whirlpool, and by the time it was filled with water, James's pastor had arrived. I was so relieved!

We all gathered in the whirlpool room, held hands, and prayed for the surgery to go well and for James to be healed. Then he was baptized. We all shed tears except for James, who beamed with pride. A few minutes later, after he had dried off and put on a fresh hospital gown, he was wheeled into surgery. Before he left, everyone once again held hands and prayed for the surgeons and nurses, and for the surgery to be a success.

And the surgery was a success. James recovered quickly and was released from the hospital within a few days. The surgeons felt very positive about the surgery. They had been able to remove the tumor, and James had no side effects as a result of having part of his brain removed. The family went home feeling great.

From that point on, James was seen at the cancer center and was not admitted back into the hospital. As far as I knew, everything was going fine.

However, one day I got a call from his mother. She apologized for not calling sooner, but she'd been so busy taking care of James, she hadn't been organized enough to make sure everyone who needed to be contacted had been. She told me James had died peacefully at home.

About two months after his release from the hospital, he had started having trouble swallowing and speaking. He'd been taken into the cancer center for more tests, and it was discovered that his tumor had some fingers that were embedded deeply in his brain. They could not be removed, because doing so would have destroyed his brain and the surgery itself would have killed him.

James's mother said that he never showed signs of anxiety or fear. He often spoke of how beautiful heaven was and that Jesus had promised to walk across the bridge with him. It was three months after his surgery when he died.

Before we hung up, his mother said, "I never stopped praying for his healing. I wanted God to heal him. I begged God to heal him. I expected that if I prayed hard enough, God would heal him. I've prayed that for so long, I'm not even sure what to pray for now." There was a long pause, and then she said, "I suppose I should start praying for even a small part of the faith James had. He never doubted."

6

Andrew

The staff of the hospital parked in a special area away from the building so that the patients, their families, and visitors could park closer. As I walked into work past the other staff cars, I noticed many of them had bumper stickers that read "Kiss your baby." I thought it was some kind of sweet reminder that new babies need kisses. I soon learned that cystic fibrosis, a very serious illness, could be discovered and early treatment begun if mothers and fathers kissed their baby and discovered he or she tasted salty. So these bumper stickers were telling parents to literally kiss their baby and, if the baby tasted salty, to get him or her checked for cystic fibrosis.

Our hospital was one of the leading research hospitals for cystic fibrosis. The lead doctor who worked in that unit had been at our hospital since she first began practicing medicine. She had dedicated her entire career to trying to extend the lives of her cystic fibrosis patients. Early diagnosis was imperative. The sooner treatment could start, the better the life expectancy the child would have. Most of the patients in the unit had been diagnosed during infancy and had spent years of their lives in and out of the hospital.

Cystic fibrosis creates a thick, sticky mucus that coats the intestinal tract and lungs of children who have it. The mucus is difficult to get rid of, so the kids and teens at our hospital spent much of their time trying to manage it. Several times a day they took a medicine cup filled with pills that helped to reduce the amount of mucus their bodies made. They had several breathing treatments each day, during which they would place a tube emitting a steam-like substance into their mouths for several minutes and then cough up mucus for what seemed like hours. They also had sessions where a little hammer was used to tap them all over their backs and chests. This would loosen the mucus and help them cough it up. They had to do a similar routine each day at home, but when the mucus built up too much, they had to come into the hospital. This happened often.

Besides making them cough, the mucus coated the patients' lungs, making the exchange of oxygen difficult. Their bodies didn't receive the oxygen they needed. Because of that, their hands were often cold and had sort of a light purple color. Mucus also coated the digestive tract, and their bodies could not absorb food very well. These kids could eat whatever they wanted whenever they wanted, and in fact, they were encouraged to eat all the time, but still they were too thin. They also had slightly clubbed fingertips. The children didn't look odd, but the purple hands, extreme thinness, and clubbed fingertips were the signs that those I was visiting had cystic fibrosis. Otherwise they looked like regular kids. Until they coughed, which was the most pitiful thing to hear.

When they had been diagnosed, their life expectancy was only a few years, but this team of medical professionals had done all in their power to make sure these kids beat the odds. They did research, they were diligent about making sure the kids took their meds and had their treatments at the correct times, and they made them eat around the clock. Some of the patients were no longer children; they had made it to their teen years because of the dedication and care of the staff, and especially because of the tireless primary doctor.

Before I visited the cystic fibrosis unit, I was warned about the no-nonsense attitude of the primary doctor and the protective nature of her staff toward the kids. Because the staff had cared for these kids since infancy, they had grown close to them. I don't think the words *professional distance* existed when it came to these kids and teens. The staff had grown to love them dearly, and they loved the staff. Their entire families loved the staff. The downside for me in all this love and care was that I was new, and no one knew yet if I could be trusted to care for these kids. I was an outsider!

Toni, the main chaplain and my supervisor, had also known these kids since they were babies. She told me I could visit any of the children in the hospital I wanted, but she asked me to wait to go to the cystic fibrosis ward until she was with me. She wanted to introduce me to the kids herself.

After a few weeks, Toni finally decided it was time to take me to the cystic fibrosis unit. When the doors opened, I found the unit was unlike any of the others. Most of the children were dressed in regular street clothes and were walking all over the place. No one was in a bed. A group of young teens was standing by the nurses' station, telling jokes and laughing loudly. Music was blaring out of the patient lounge, and the children and teens were dancing and playing cards and painting pictures. They were joking around, stealing each other's baseball caps, and riding wheelchairs for fun up and down the halls. The unit looked more like a youth group room at church than a hospital ward. Rather than walk to a child or teen and tell them it was time for their meds, a nurse would just holler down the hall for one of these kids to come get their medicine.

Toni was popular with the kids. I could immediately tell that she loved them and they loved her. They ran to hug her when she entered the unit, and she asked them all kinds of questions about things that were going on in their lives. They showed her the new toys they had gotten and pictures from the latest school dance. She asked about their parents and siblings. It felt less like a visit from a chaplain and more like a family reunion.

I was introduced to all the kids, who were welcoming and outgoing toward me, as kids usually are. Then she introduced me to the staff. They were nice enough but too busy to really engage in small talk. And last, she introduced me to the doctor of the unit. I had heard so much about this woman and had wondered what she looked like. She was older, only a tiny bit taller than me, and looked more like a grandmother than the top research doctor I had expected to meet.

She wasn't warm to me in the least. She shook my hand, leaned in close, and said, "These kids have a hard battle ahead of them. They're brave and they have positive attitudes. They need both to outlive the odds. Don't come in here if you can't bring them hope. They don't need negative energy."

Toni assured her that I had a positive attitude and would not do anything to dash the hopes of these kids. I smiled an agreeing smile, but the doctor glared at me. I could tell she didn't believe us.

I wasn't eager to go back to the cystic fibrosis unit after that, for fear the staff would intimidate me and I would run into that doctor again, but it was my job to visit as many children as I could each day. Believe me, I tried to fill my days in other parts of the hospital, but the time came when the only patients I hadn't seen were the ones in the cystic fibrosis ward. I walked to the unit, took a deep breath, and went in.

There they were, all of the kids laughing, dancing, joking with the staff, helping themselves to the food in the staff room, and paying absolutely no attention to me. I was unsure of where to start when I heard coughing coming from one of the rooms. No one else seemed to be worried about this child, but it sounded to me like he was coughing so long and so hard that he might pass out before he could take a breath.

I went to the door of the room and peeked in. A tall, thin boy with blond hair was sitting on the bed, crossed-legged and coughing so hard that his entire body was purple. He motioned for me to come in, which surprised me. He had been coughing into a small plastic dish that he handed to me and asked if I minded dumping it while he started coughing into another one. I took the dish into his bathroom, flushed the mucus down the toilet, and asked him if I was supposed to wash it. He laughed through his coughs and said, "No, throw it away. I have about eighteen more of them over here."

Finally the poor teen stopped coughing. I thought he might be upset or embarrassed to have coughed up mucus in front of me, but I soon learned that these kids had been coughing so long and were so used to it that they were no longer fazed by it at all. It was just part of life.

I introduced myself, and he told me his name was Andrew. He was fifteen years old. By the end of our first visit, I knew a lot about him. He had been diagnosed with cystic fibrosis as a baby. His dad had left him and his mother because he could not accept that his son wasn't perfect. His mom worked hard all day and visited him every evening she possibly could. He was the oldest child in the unit and very proud of that. He told me all about cystic fibrosis, what the treatments were like, what it felt like to cough for twenty minutes at a time, and all about the research they were doing to try to cure it. He had been part of many of the research experiments and believed that he would live to be an adult.

There was something very special about Andrew. He had spent most of his life fighting with and trying to get along with his disease, his father had abandoned him, and he wasn't sure how long he would live, yet he was sweet and open and had a genuine smile on his face every time I visited him. There was no sign of fear or despair in him. It was clear in many ways that not only had his attitude helped him live longer than anyone expected, but it had also set the tone for the younger kids. They weren't afraid because Andrew wasn't afraid. They would live until their teen years because Andrew had!

I started visiting Andrew regularly and quickly realized why the cystic fibrosis unit didn't need a chaplain: they had Andrew. Each day he made the rounds to every child in the unit. He asked them questions and listened while they answered. When they were coughing hard, he would quietly sit next to them, rubbing their backs until they stopped. When they had a question about meds or about a treatment, they would often ask Andrew before asking their nurse. When they were afraid, Andrew would be the first one who knew. In fact, he would tell me who needed a visit from me most each day. When I would tell a child or teen that Andrew had sent me, they would open right up and trust me immediately.

Before you think Andrew was a saint, I should share that he was obsessed with women. He said inappropriate things to cute nurses and drew sexy pictures of women in a notebook beside his bed. He told me that the reason he was determined to outlive the odds was because he loved women and wanted to get married as soon as he could! It broke my heart to hear him talk of getting married; I knew that while he had outlived the original diagnosis, children with cystic fibrosis did not make it to adulthood. Thankfully, they often do today, but back then it was fairly certain that he would not.

Over time Andrew and I became very close. I would often save his visit for the last one of my day because I knew it would be a good visit. I saw him each time he was in the hospital for the entire three years I worked there. He told me a lot about what it was like to be an only child of a single mother. He could not go to school because the coughing was distracting to the other children, so he spent most of his time at home. A private teacher assigned by his school district came each day for an hour to teach him, check his homework, and assign him more. Other than her visits, he was usually home alone. He loved his mother, missed her, and longed to have her around more. I often wondered if his determination and desire to get married as soon as he could was really because he needed someone to spend time with and break his loneliness and isolation.

Andrew was a great artist. Even though the content of his artwork was usually provocatively dressed women, the pictures were well done. He used a pen-and-ink style in full color. I have no idea how many hours he spent on each drawing, but it must have been a long time. Each one was intricately crafted.

One day when I visited Andrew, he was eager for me to look at his newest drawing. I sat down in the chair next to his bed, and he opened his notebook. I was expecting to see another picture of a woman, but instead it was a colorful collection of hearts. There were colors streaming out of the hearts and colliding and creating new hearts. Every inch of the page was covered with these hearts, which were so full of colorful energy you could almost see them move.

"This is beautiful!" I said. "When did you draw this, and where are the women?"

Andrew laughed. Then he grew serious and looked me deeply in the eyes. "Did I ever tell you that I'm Baptist?"

"No," I said.

"Well, I am, and at my church, all these people 'get moved by the Spirit' and speak in tongues and do all this nutty stuff. All this time my mom has dragged me there, and I thought these people were nuts. Sometimes I would make myself start coughing so we could leave! And then all of a sudden, last night, I think I got 'moved by the Spirit' or something like that. I heard God's voice. No, I felt God's voice or something. Or maybe I felt the love of heaven. I think it *was* heaven! I mean, it was God, and God's love stretches all the way from heaven to earth, doesn't it?

"I felt love like I have never felt it before. It filled my whole body, and I had to draw these hearts because if I hadn't, I felt like I would have been so filled with love I would explode! God's love is so beautiful. I mean, I'm trying to draw it, but I can't. You can't imagine how I feel inside. And somehow I have to draw it so the other children here can see it and never be afraid again.

"When I die, when any of us die, this love will be waiting for us. And you can get it on earth too, but only in tiny pieces.

When I get married, the love will be there, but it will only be a tiny piece of God's love for us in heaven. There is no love on earth that will be like the love in heaven, but earthly love is important because it shows us—it lets us feel the love of God that we'll be surrounded by even more strongly in heaven."

He started to laugh. "Do I sound like a nut?" he asked.

"No, you sound like a prophet," I replied.

From then on, Andrew continued filling his notebooks with drawings, but they were no longer drawings of women. They were of hearts with colors pouring out of them and entwining with one another. He drew them in his notebooks, he doodled them on napkins, and he showed them to everyone. He wasn't trying to convert people, and he rarely told them that his pictures were trying to capture God's love. He simply shared them with others and let the drawings say everything that needed to be or could be spoken.

One time he shared with me a picture of himself with a woman on his wedding day. They stood beneath an arch made of those colorful hearts. I felt sad for Andrew because I doubted he would ever be able to marry, but I didn't share my sadness with him. If he wanted to get married, who was I to tell him the truth? I had learned that the words of the doctor during my first visit to the unit were true. These kids needed hope, and if Andrew was hoping to get married, then I would let him hope!

Andrew was still living when I left the hospital to work for a church. I hated to tell him goodbye, and we promised to stay in touch, but life got busy and soon he stopped writing me. A few years later, I was at the grocery store and ran into his doctor. She didn't remember me, but I remembered her. I reintroduced myself and asked how things at the hospital were, then asked about Andrew. Tears filled her eyes, and she told me that he had recently died. He was twenty-one years old.

"I recall how much he always wanted to be married, and I'm sorry he didn't get to," I said.

She smiled and said, "Oh, he did get married. A nice girl when he was nineteen. They were married two years! I was at the wedding—front row!" She smiled, wiped the tears that were rolling down her cheeks, and walked away. It was the first and only time I ever saw her cry.

When I returned home, I looked at the picture of the colorful hearts I had hanging on my bedroom wall. Andrew had drawn it for me, and I loved it so much that I'd framed it. I looked at the beautiful colors and the love that poured from the picture. I knew with certainty that these hearts of love were surrounding Andrew now in heaven, and I thanked God that Andrew had been given such great loves: the love of heaven, the love of marriage, and the love of the most caring doctor I had ever met.

7

Jeffery

One of the best parts of my job as a chaplain was that I was blessed to work with my supervisor and the other student chaplains. While I worked at the hospital, there were times when my supervisor and I were the only two chaplains and other times when we had additional students from the seminary working with us.

Janna was already working at the hospital when I arrived. She was one of the funniest, down-to-earth people I had ever met, and she was a great storyteller. My favorite stories were ones of the care packages her grandmother would send her. Her grandmother would sometimes send homemade cookies or jelly but had no idea how to pack them, so the cookies would be broken and the jelly would be all over the place. I loved when these packages would arrive because Janna would always tell me about them in the most entertaining way.

My favorite care package story was of the time when her grandmother was worried that Janna wasn't eating enough, so she sent her a pound of bacon. She simply placed a pound of bacon, fresh from the farm, in a box and mailed it. The package arrived completely covered in grease and smelling horrible. I don't ever remember laughing harder in my entire life. I'm not sure if I laughed so hard because the story was so funny or because of Janna's laughing, hooting, and hollering as she told it!

No matter what had happened to a child or what a family was facing, Janna could always bring humor into the situation. She didn't make light of the circumstances but rather used her humor as a way of helping herself and others cope with stress and sorrow. The hospital staff especially loved her because she would always lighten the mood after a stressful event.

She wasn't always funny, though. She was working hard in seminary, and she was serious about taking care of the children and families we served. She was a great chaplain. She could walk into a room, and through her warm personality and sense of humor paired with her storytelling, she could gain the trust of families in a matter of moments.

Janna and I would often eat lunch together and share stories, both about our personal lives and about the families and patients we were working with. It was nice to have a confidant. Janna liked all the families she worked with, but there was one preteen, Jeffery, whom she was especially attached to. She told me about him almost every time she visited him, and it really bothered her that he was sick.

I knew she was especially attached to Jeffery because she never laughed when she spoke of him. Jeffery had been diagnosed as a child with a disease called sickle cell anemia, which is passed down through parents who each carry the gene, especially those of African or Mediterranean descent. People who have sickle cell anemia have misshapen red blood cells.

Rather than being round like healthy blood cells, these cells are crescent shaped. This makes the red blood cells fragile, so infections are common. The life expectancy now is much better, but for Jeffery, living until he was twenty-one would have been the best diagnosis his family could hope for.

Sickle cell anemia is a very painful disease. Patients experience what is called a "crisis," during which they can have swelling of their feet and hands, abdominal pain, shortness of breath, and bone pain. Jeffery would often have to come to the hospital when he was in crisis so that he could receive stronger pain medications through an IV than he could at home. Most of the time when he was in our hospital, he was in severe pain and so uncomfortable that he rarely spoke.

Jeffery was a tall twelve-year-old and very thin, which made him seem even taller. He was one of the only children whose feet stuck out the end of his bed. He hardly ever smiled and mostly worked on puzzles or made models of cars or planes. He didn't complain, groan, or cry, but it was obvious that staying quiet and focusing on the puzzles or models was the only way he could keep from doing so.

I knew of Jeffery mostly because of Janna's stories. I rarely visited him because he was special to her and she visited so often that I didn't need to. But I did come to see his family once on a Sunday afternoon.

I had been called in early to sit with a mother whose child had been brought into the emergency room for a near drowning. We were not sure if he would pull through, so the staff asked me to be with his mother until her family could be contacted and get to the hospital. The child ended up being stabilized fairly quickly, and it was soon apparent that he would live. He was moved to the intensive care unit for an overnight stay. After I finished helping the mom make her contacts to family members and settle into the intensive care waiting room, I decided to walk around the hospital and make a few visits. My adrenaline had been pumping, and I wasn't ready to go home.

Hospitals are quiet places on Sunday afternoons. The staffing is minimal and playrooms are not open, so it has an almost eerie quietness. I walked up and down the hallways, stopping by several rooms to say hello and check on families.

All of a sudden I heard laughing—lots of laughing—coming from a room down the hall. And I could smell fried chicken, green beans, and corn bread. I walked toward the laughter and the smell and discovered that all the fun was happening in Jeffery's room. It was a small room and was absolutely packed with people who had clearly come from church. They were dressed in suits and dresses, and several of the women had white gloves and hats on.

I grew up in Kentucky, so I recognized this scene. It was a wonderful Sunday dinner at Granny's. But instead of having the dinner at Granny's home, it was happening in a hospital room.

The scene immediately took me back to my own granny's dinners. I walked in and said hello, knowing that they would invite me to stay and eat—everyone is welcome at Sunday dinner! I wasn't disappointed. They immediately handed me a plate and told me to eat up. I almost cried, because I hadn't had my granny's cooking since she died when I was in fourth grade, and now here it was on my own plate!

There was more food than anyone could eat. Chicken, fried perfectly, golden brown and crispy; green beans that had cooked all night; corn bread—the really thick kind that tastes like sweet cake topped with honey and butter; and even a red metal Coca-Cola cooler filled with bottles of Coke, just like my Granny always had on her back porch at every dinner. We ate and laughed, and before long I felt like I had known these people for my entire life.

After dinner the praying started. The family circled around Jeffery and prayed one by one. Their prayers were not the like the prayers I grew up hearing in the United Methodist Church. The family began quietly, almost in a whisper, with a retelling of a Bible story, reminding God and everyone listening of his power. One person retold the story of Moses and how God took the people out of Egypt and into the Promised Land. Another person told the story of Daniel surviving in the lions' den. Still another told the story of the three children of God who were thrown into the fiery furnace and who were protected by an angel.

As each story was told, the speaker's voice level increased, and then they began reminding God that if he could save the people with Moses, then God could save Jeffery from this illness. If Daniel was saved, God could surely save Jeffery. If the children of God survived a fiery furnace, then God could clearly stop Jeffery's pain.

The person speaking not only got louder, they started to almost sing as they spoke. The song was rhythmic and beautiful, and as the person praying begin to sing, the others would chant and hum along. It was if a psalm had been composed at that very moment and was as holy as any psalm I had ever read from the Bible.

Jeffery sat in his bed with his eyes closed, praying along with them. He believed their words and prayed that these heartfelt prayers would be answered.

It was a special time. Because I had shared Sunday dinner with this family, I felt bonded to them in some way. I began to stop by and say hello each time Jeffery was in the hospital.

One day I came by and found his room dark. Jeffery was asleep and his mother was sitting next to his bed, crying. She held Jeffery's hand in both of hers. As soon as I walked in, she asked me to sit down on the other side of the bed. I sat down and she started to pray. It wasn't a prayer like the ones given at Sunday dinner. It was a quiet prayer, almost a mantra. She whispered to God over and over, "Lord, you have the power to heal my son. Heal my son."

Her tears fell as she prayed and rocked back and forth, holding tightly to Jeffery's hand. Then she looked up at me and said, "Why won't God answer my prayers? Why does he need my son? Why would he let my son suffer like this? God has all the power! I don't understand."

I said nothing. What could I say? I simply took his other hand in mine and sat quietly, watching her pray and rock. I sat there silently, asking God the same question that Jeffery's mother did: *Why?*

After several minutes, Jeffery began to stir. His mother wiped her eyes, put a smile on her face, and asked him what he needed. He was thirsty. She got a cup of water, placed her arm behind his head, and helped him drink. It was such a loving and sensitive moment. I felt like I was watching Michelangelo's statue of the *Pietà* come to life as I watched this mother holding her son in her arms, trying to accept God's will.

We chatted for a few minutes about nothing, trying to regain our composure, and then I left. I told Janna about the visit. It was so heartbreaking for both of us to watch a mother so desperately want her son to be healed, and knowing that since there was no cure for sickle cell anemia, only a miracle could heal him.

The interesting thing about Jeffery's mom was that day to day, when I visited, she never showed any signs of sadness or doubt. She laughed, told stories, and lifted the spirits of Jeffery and their family. It was only on rare visits, when she was alone and he was asleep, that she would show any signs of distress. She knew that he needed her to be hopeful. She knew that if she started to show signs of fear or hopelessness, his anxiety would increase. So she played her role of hopeful and fearless mother better than probably any mother I had ever met.

As time went on and Jeffery had more pain and had to spend more time in the hospital because of crises, his mother would speak openly to Janna and me about her disappointment in God for not caring for her son. She shared with us that she had grown up in the church. She had never missed a Sunday service in her life except when Jeffery was in the hospital, and even then she had read her Bible and prayed for a full hour. God had been with her family as she grew up as a poor child in the South and had supplied their every need. He had given her a good husband, a wonderful family, and a home to live in and had never let them want for anything. She had never doubted God's love for her.

But now she felt her faith start to slip away. For the first time in her life, she doubted God's love. Sometimes she even doubted his existence. It was terrifying for her to have feelings of doubt. She knew God was all that was keeping her going. Life without him was unimaginable for her, and yet she wondered whether he was real or not. And if God was real, where was he when she was begging him for help?

Jeffery continued to come into the hospital on a regular basis. The times between visits, which previously had been months apart, were often weeks or days apart now. Janna and her husband were celebrating their tenth wedding anniversary and had planned a trip to celebrate. She asked me to watch Jeffery's family closely if he should come in while she was away. I promised her I would.

Jeffery came in a day or so after Janna left town. As promised, I stopped in to see him every day that I worked. He was in a lot of pain—it seemed like more than usual. The stress showed on his face and was mirrored on his mother's.

Once when I stopped by to visit, the room was filled with family members. There must have been ten people in the room, and Jeffery, to my surprise, was sitting up, smiling, and talking. I had never seen him smile and be talkative, but now he was charming and charismatic. This explained why he had so many cards from the girls at his school always filling his bulletin board. This was a Jeffery I had never gotten the opportunity to see.

One of his uncles had brought him a toy bow and arrow set. The target was hung on the bulletin board in front of the cards, and several of the men in the room, including Jeffery, were taking turns shooting the arrows at the board. The arrows had suction cups on the ends, so sometimes they would stick and other times they would bounce off. The men were shooting arrows, laughing, and coming up with theory after theory about how to hold the bow and how far to pull the string to make the arrows stick to the target. I loved watching Jeffery talk, laugh, and enjoy himself so much.

When it was his turn, he held the bow up and pulled back the arrow, but then he was distracted. He looked to the right side of the room and said, "Now? You want me to come and live with Jesus now?"

There was silence in the room—stunned silence.

Jeffery looked at the target on the wall, then turned back toward the right and said, "Of course. I'm ready." The bow and arrow dropped from his hands, his head fell back onto his pillow, and he was completely still.

The room was silent. None of us knew what had happened. I ran out and grabbed a nurse. She came in looking puzzled, got out her stethoscope, and listened for a heartbeat. As she listened, we all began to wake up from the daze that had filled the room, and slowly, one by one, each of us realized that Jeffery had died.

The family had signed a Do Not Resuscitate order, so they didn't try to restart Jeffery's heart. The nurse might have announced that he had died, but I don't recall it. One by one, each family member stepped up to the bed, formed a circle, and began to pray. This time their stories were of times such as the death of Moses after he had completed his mission of leading the Israelites; of Elijah and how the heavenly chariot carried him to God; and of Christ, who died on the cross only to be resurrected and made the King of heaven.

Just like at Sunday dinner, their voices got louder and they began to sing. The psalm they created was a mixture of rejoicing and deep sorrow. I began to hum along and looked over at Jeffery's mother. She had her eyes shut tightly and was saying over and over, "God, I thank you for being merciful to my son. God, I thank you."

A deep holiness filled the room, created both by God's presence and by the grateful hearts of these faith-filled people who were singing their prayers to him. I wondered if Jeffery's mom still had any doubts about God's existence. I had no doubts. I had never felt holiness like this.

Jeffery's mother opened her eyes and looked at me. I felt embarrassed, afraid that she had felt my stare and sense of wonder. She looked me straight in the eyes and smiled just the smallest smile, nodded her head, and said, "The Lord was merciful to my son. God had great mercy on my son. I suppose it won't be long now till I will join him in heaven." She closed her eyes and continued to praise God for his mercy. Then she began to quietly sing an old hymn I used to sing as a child, and as she sang, her voice grew strong:

> "In the sweet by and by,   ·
> We shall meet on that beautiful shore;
> In the sweet by and by,
> We shall meet on that beautiful shore."[1]

I knew that her doubts were no longer there.

One of the most difficult calls I have ever made was to Janna to tell her that Jeffery had died. I didn't really need to tell her. She was still on her trip, so as soon as she heard my voice, she knew the only reason I called was for something important.

I shared the story of Jeffery's peaceful but sudden death, and she was quiet. There was nothing funny she could say and no humor she could find to make the news less painful. We hung up, and I assume she wept, as I did.

I sat there thinking about how many times I had read Bible stories. Hearing those stories not just retold but literally prayed by these faithful people, and watching the way that the stories themselves ministered to them better than any chaplain ever could have, I realized how powerful the Word of God can be.

1. Sanford F. Bennett and Joseph P. Webster, "In the Sweet By and By," 1868.

8

Catherine

One morning as I looked over the files, I saw we had a new admittance, Catherine. I wanted to drop by and see her first thing in the morning before I started visiting my usual kids and families and lost track of the time.

I went to her door, knocked, and entered. I had read on the admittance list that she was suffering from a liver disorder and was waiting for a liver transplant. I had never seen anyone who needed a liver before, so I was shocked to see Catherine for the first time.

She was five years old but looked as if she were three. She was very round, like a pudgy toddler. I'm not sure if she was short for her age or if the water retention from her disease made her look short, but she was definitely rounder than she was tall. When I entered, she was sitting alone on her bed, cross-legged and smiling. She had thick, curly blonde hair, and she almost looked more like a Shirley Temple doll than a child.

The thing I found most fascinating and surprising about Catherine was the color of her skin. Every inch of this child was yellow, like my skin would look when my mother used iodine on a cut. It was as if someone had dipped Catherine into yellow iodine to make her better. But I knew that wasn't the case. This discoloring was the result of her liver not working properly. I wasn't a doctor or nurse, but from one glance I could tell that this little girl was very ill.

There was a nurse in the room who must have seen the look of shock on my face, even though I thought I had masked it well with a little smile. She pulled me to the corner of the room and said in a whisper, "Little girls whose livers don't work turn yellow."

"What exactly does the liver do?" I asked.

She responded, "Everything! You're the chaplain here—you'd better start praying she gets a new one pretty soon!"

I went back over to Catherine's bed and tried to talk to her. She was a pleasant little girl with a darling smile, but it seemed to be frozen on her face. It was clear that she was sitting so still with that smile because it took too much energy to move. She was frozen in a comfortable position, and the thought of moving even the smallest muscle required more energy than she had. I decided to just sit next to her for a while.

I smiled and she sat, frozen yet present. My heart broke to see this little girl so sick. I prayed silently that she would receive the liver she needed.

The rest of the day was filled with visits to my usual kids and spending time in the playroom with the staff and kids. It was a good day, but I could not get Catherine off my mind. I kept seeing her sitting so still and lifeless on her bed with that smile. I imagined how lively she would be if she felt better. She hadn't spoken to me, but I could tell she was a bright, active child who was trapped in a body that so badly needed a new liver.

Later that day I met in the outer office with my supervisor. We were drinking tea and eating candy bars, and I was filling her in on my day. I talked about all the funny and cute things the kids did and then told her about Catherine. She knew Catherine, who had been in the hospital several times before. She had met the little girl when she was first diagnosed with liver failure and had been called to the emergency room several times.

"She's a strong kid!" Toni told me. "I can't tell you how many times she's nearly died, but she always pulls through. I never know what to pray for when it comes to transplants."

I had no idea what she was talking about. I knew how to pray. I wanted this child to get a liver! I was clear about my prayers.

She could see the judgmental look on my face and began to explain how the organ transplant system worked. A person waiting for an organ is placed on a transplant list. The only organs that can be harvested are from people who die suddenly and are healthy. Most of the organs used for transplants come from young healthy people who are killed in some kind of accident such as a car or motorcycle wreck. She personally had a hard time praying for a child—even one as precious as Catherine—to receive an organ because it meant indirectly praying for some other healthy person to die. For Catherine to receive a liver, someone had to die. The joy her family would experience would come at the cost of another family enduring horrible pain.

My judgmental attitude dissolved, and I understood the complexity of the situation. Up until this point, prayer had seemed so simple to me. You needed something and you asked God for it. This was the first time I had ever considered that what I wanted—what I needed—could mean someone else's suffering or pain.

This realization deeply affected me. I began to pause before each prayer I uttered, trying to think of any negative ramifications that might result from my request. I reminded myself that God didn't have to answer every prayer and tried to stop analyzing every word I spoke.

Finally, after finding prayer to be way more complicated than it had been, I began to say a prayer I had never really used much before. It was the one Jesus spoke in the Garden of Gethsemane the night of his arrest: "Father, if you are willing, take this cup from me; yet not my will, but yours be done" (Luke 22:42 NIV). Each time I would think of Catherine or walk past her room, I would say that prayer: "Father, if you are willing, let Catherine receive the liver she needs to live. But it is your will, not mine. I trust your wisdom."

It was a different prayer, though, that I spoke when her mother asked for prayer. Kate was a single mother and the sole breadwinner for her and Catherine. She had to work during the days, which meant Catherine spent much of her time without an adult in the room. Kate suffered from guilt about this and would come straight from work each day to spend the evening and nights beside her daughter. She often looked worn out and frazzled, but you would never have known it by the way she treated Catherine. She was patient, attentive, and sweet to her daughter. They would both soak up their time together, reading books, telling stories, and snuggling. It was one of the few times of the day where Catherine smiled and talked. I wondered if part of her stillness during the days was a way of preserving her energy for her time with her mom.

I didn't get to see Kate often. I worked during the days, so I was often gone before she arrived. On the rare occasions when she and I did see each other, she would ask me to pray. I was torn. Did I pray the prayer I had carefully taught myself to pray, asking God's will to be done—or did I pray the prayer this mother needed to hear?

I looked at Kate. I knew that for her, in this one moment, she had as much faith in my prayer as the woman who had touched the hem of Christ's garment had in his ability to heal her. I prayed as hard as I could that Catherine would be given a liver, be healed, and live. And the strange part is that I meant every word of it! In that moment of such desperate need, I prayed straight from my heart the prayer that Kate carried in her heart. I understood intercessory prayer—praying on behalf of another person—better in that moment than I ever have since. From then on, I still prayed my prayer of God's will privately, but I never hesitated to pray for a liver when praying with Catherine or her mother.

Catherine got stronger and went home. It was only a few weeks, though, before she was back. I went to see her, and there she was just like before, sitting on her bed, looking like a Shirley Temple doll that had been dipped in yellow iodine. She was puffier than she had been, and I was told the puffiness was a result of toxins, which the liver usually breaks down, building up in her little body.

One day I asked her why she always sat up rather than lie down and rest. She told me that her skin hurt and she didn't like the feel of the sheets on it. If she sat up, she didn't have to feel the sheets.

I tried to visit Catherine every day, especially since her mother was working so much of the time. We never spoke much, but she loved books, so I would bring books with me and read them to her. It would break my heart that she enjoyed hearing the stories so much, because I could tell it hurt her to smile sometimes, yet she could not help but giggle at the funny parts. She was such an ill child and yet so normal, still laughing at silly children's books and enjoying finding the hidden pictures in mystery picture books.

The nurses and doctors began to worry. Catherine was getting worse and there was a not a liver to be found. She no longer had the strength to sit up in her bed and began lying down. Her color was now bright yellow and her lips began to crack. I could tell she was dying more and more each time I visited. Her mother took off work and began spending time at the hospital around the clock.

The staff met with Catherine's mother and told her that unless there was a miracle, Catherine would die within a few days, maybe even within hours. They called me to sit with Kate, and we prayed for a miracle. We prayed for a liver, but also that God would make Catherine's liver start working again. It didn't, and things began looking worse than ever. At this point, even if a liver became available, she was most likely not strong enough to make it through the operation.

Hopelessness set in for everyone. There was very little the hospital staff could do. They changed Catherine's IV fluids, tried to get her to eat something, gave her tender baths, and changed her sheets. Other than that, we waited for her death to arrive.

The first day passed and she was still alive. The second day passed and she was still alive. Day by day she grew weaker, her discomfort grew, but she held on. There were many theories floating around the staff about why she wasn't letting go. Some of them thought that perhaps she was afraid to disappoint her mother by dying, so they asked Kate to tell her that it was okay to go to heaven and that she would see her there someday. Kate did as they asked. She could not bear to see her child hurt much longer.

Another theory was that Catherine was in pain and was hanging on for fear that the pain would be worse when she died. They upped her pain medication, and the pain stopped. Still Catherine hung on. It was pitiful to see this child hang on to life so desperately. There is a point in life when it becomes obvious that there are worse things than dying. Everyone, including Catherine's mother, was hoping that she would let go and be rid of her pain and suffering. But Catherine hung on!

Early one morning I was paged to Catherine's room. I ran there, thinking perhaps she had died, but when I arrived her nurse was waiting by the door. She told me that while she was caring for Catherine, Catherine had been talking in her sleep and asking for her father. The nurse thought she was crying out to God, her heavenly Father, but she wasn't sure and wanted me to see if Catherine would tell me.

I went into Catherine's room. She was asleep, but her mother was awake. I told Kate what the nurse had observed, and she shared that she had also heard Catherine calling out for her father. I asked her if she thought Catherine might have been calling out to God.

"I'm not sure," Kate said. "We pray but we don't go to church often, especially since she's been sick. But she doesn't know her biological father, so I think she must have been calling to God."

I waited for Catherine to wake up, and when she did I asked her if she remembered calling out for her father.

"Is he here?" she asked. "Is he here? My father?"

"Do you mean God?" I asked.

"No, my father. My daddy—my real one. Is he here? I need to see him. I need to tell him something!"

I looked over at Kate, who had a look of something between panic and shock on her face. She shook her head and then looked at Catherine, who was now sitting up and telling us that we needed to get her daddy for her.

I took Kate out in the hall and asked if there was any way we could find her father. At first she said no, but after a few minutes, she told me that Catherine's father had abandoned Kate while she was still pregnant, though he did contact her every so often asking about Catherine. He had never asked to meet her or to be part of her life. Kate had never told her daughter about him, and she had never asked. The father had not been told that Catherine was ill.

Kate dug in her purse and found a slip of paper with the last number he had contacted her from written on it. We found her a private waiting area with a phone, and she called him. He said he would come but that it would take him a couple of days to get there because he had moved out of state.

Catherine was told that her father was coming. Her breath was labored at this point, and it was painful to watch her struggle to breathe. She stopped communicating with us, and it was difficult to tell if she still heard us. She didn't eat, and she slept nearly all the time. Still, she hung on for the two days it took her father to drive to the hospital.

When he arrived, I felt a mixture of joy and disgust, and several of the staff felt the same. We had all grown to love Catherine so much, it was inconceivable to us that he had never even taken the time to meet her. I must admit, though, that when he came walking up to the unit where Catherine was, I could not help but feel pity for him. He was tense and visibly shaken. He had never seen his daughter, he hadn't cared for her, and now she was dying. I have no idea if it was guilt, remorse, or plain old fear I saw on his face and in his eyes, but it was pitiful. He was a humble and broken man about to visit his dying daughter.

Kate was sitting by her daughter's bed, and she came out into the hall when Catherine's father arrived. He smiled and tried to hug her, but she pushed him away and said, "I'm sorry I didn't contact you sooner. I mean, I wasn't sure if you'd want to know or how involved in all of this you wanted to be." An awkward silence followed, and finally Kate broke it. "Do you want to see her?"

Before Catherine's father had even a moment to answer, a nurse who was standing by stepped closer to him and explained, "She's a very sick little girl. Don't be disappointed if she doesn't recognize you or talk to you."

He nodded that he understood, walked into the room, and nervously sat down next to his daughter. At first he held her hand and then began to stroke her hair. And then he asked, "Can I hold her?"

The nurse moved a large recliner next to the bed so he could sit in it. Then she and Kate placed Catherine in his arms. He began to cry and then to sob, rocking her as a new father might rock his newborn.

Catherine opened her eyes for a moment and said, "Daddy." It was as if she had known him all her life. He was speechless, and he sat there rocking her harder and crying. She opened her eyes again and said, "Daddy, I have something to tell you. God told me to tell you before I die that he forgives you. I forgive you too, Daddy."

No one said a word. He continued rocking his daughter for about ten minutes. Catherine closed her eyes. The nurse didn't tell anyone what she suspected but simply told the man that his daughter needed to rest. She laid Catherine back in the hospital bed. She waited a few moments and then took the child's pulse and checked her heart with a stethoscope. She quietly told us that Catherine had died.

I thought about all the prayers I had spoken in that room. I thought about all the things I had asked God for. I had asked for Catherine to be healed and to be given a new liver, but never once had I prayed for what she really needed—to be held by her father. God's will had been done.

9

Joyce

I was first drawn to working with children who were very sick because I had read *On Death and Dying* by Elisabeth Kübler-Ross and had been amazed and moved by her stories of her work with dying children. She wrote about their deep spirituality and their bravery. As I read, I pictured these children in my mind and imagined what each one looked like. I thought they would be similar to very ill people in movies, which was the closest I had ever come to seeing someone with a terminal illness.

I loved the movie *Love Story*. Ali MacGraw had been so lovely as she died, wrapped in the arms of handsome Ryan O'Neal, her long black hair flowing over the two of them. It was sad and deeply moving. So as I read Elisabeth Kübler-Ross's book, I would imagine what it would be like to be the chaplain at the bedsides of these children as they died.

Not everything in the movies was unrealistic. Death is sad, yet there is a beauty to it sometimes. But perhaps *beauty* is too strong a word. There is a quiet mystery to it, and at the moment of death, many times a peaceful feeling will fill the room that makes even the most distressed family members accept what is happening to their loved one.

Because of movies, I had imagined people would get sick and then slowly and steadily become more ill until they died. But I discovered the dying process was more of a roller coaster ride than a steady decline. A child would be okay one day and extremely ill the next. I would think they were surely going to die, and they would bounce back and be just fine for a few more days or months. It was much more unpredictable than I had imagined.

And the effect illness has on the body is rarely shown in movies. The cancer children I worked with had bruises on their bodies and sores in their mouths, and they had lost their hair before they died. They were still beautiful, but not in the Hollywood way.

Joyce was the first of many children with cancer I encountered. I first met her when I was going into the chaplains' office to chart some notes in the logbook of visitations we had done. Each time we met with a family, we would record it in a book so we could remember their situation and have it to look back on when they returned. I walked into the office, not expecting anyone to be there, and as I opened the logbook, out of the corner of my eye I saw something move. I screamed and the person screamed back.

She was a preteen, probably twelve years old, and she had a perfectly round face, puffy hands painted with bright pink nail polish, and a multicolored scarf on her head. I knew from looking at her that she must be receiving some kind of cancer treatments. I looked a little closer and noticed that she had no hair on her face at all. Even her eyelashes and eyebrows had fallen out. She had on huge gold earrings and lots of jewelry. I could tell she liked to look pretty, as all girls do; she wasn't about to let cancer stop her from accessorizing!

After we realized we had scared each other out of our wits, we both broke into laughter. Then she said, "You must be another new student chaplain." Immediately I knew she had been a patient at the hospital for a long time.

She asked if Toni was around, and when I said she hadn't come in yet, she went to Toni's desk, opened the top drawer, and took out a pad of paper and a pen. Clearly this had not been her first visit to this office. She wrote a note that read, "Hey—I was here!" with a huge heart drawn around the words. She didn't sign it. She smiled at what she had created, walked out of the office, and then peeked her head back in to say a quick goodbye.

When Toni arrived, I told her about the girl who had left her a note, and she read it, smiled, and said, "You met Joyce. I love that kid so much." She went on to tell me the story of Joyce. She had been just a little girl when she was first diagnosed with cancer, and she had survived the odds and was doing very well. Because of her type of cancer, though, she had to be on meds that often made her puffy, so she looked overweight. She also had a type of cancer that tended to go into remission for a while and then come back. The meds were designed to keep it from coming back, but when it did return, she would have to go through another round of chemotherapy.

Toni invited me to come with her to find Joyce. She knew right where to go, and we walked—or I should say, nearly ran—to the outpatient cancer treatment center. She waved at the nurses at the front desk and walked straight back into the chemotherapy room. As soon as Joyce saw her, she lit up.

Toni smiled bigger than I had ever seen her smile and yelled, "How the heck are you?"

They immediately started talking about everything. Joyce told Toni about school and hating math because she could not understand algebra. She talked about her new boyfriend and how cute he was. Toni told her about her new house and how stressful it was choosing the furniture.

I watched the two of them talk, and it reminded me more of two girlfriends at a slumber party or an aunt with her beloved niece than the professional relationship of a chaplain and a sick child. To watch Joyce laugh and chat, you would have thought she'd never had a worry in her life, let alone that she was plugged into a machine giving her chemotherapy. It was darling to watch, but I felt a bit out of place, so I made up an excuse and left the two of them to get caught up without being observed by me.

Each time Joyce would come into the hospital, I would call Toni and let her know. She would drop what she was doing and dash off to see her young friend. Sometimes when Toni wasn't there, Joyce would sit in the chaplains' office and chat with me. We spent most of our time talking about fashion and movie stars.

Joyce was really good at making herself look stylish, even with cancer. She hid the extra weight she carried by layering her outfits, and she hid the fact that she was bald by wearing colorful scarves and hats. She always had on large, stylish earrings, rings, and bracelets, as well as fun, colorful socks. She became my fashion stylist. If I had somewhere to go and needed to look nice, she would help me decide just what I should wear and always had suggestions about how I could make myself look a little better. She really knew fashion and was so much fun to talk to!

She was also always reading the latest celebrity gossip magazines. She knew which Hollywood stars were together and which ones were breaking up. She knew who was cast in which movies and had already read the reviews of new movies before I ever had a chance to, so she would consult with me about what movie was worth seeing and which ones I should skip. In essence, she became my weekend planner. She would tell me where to go and what to wear.

I looked forward to the times I would see Joyce and enjoyed them so much, but sometimes I felt guilty after our visits, because rarely did we talk about her cancer or even herself. We talked about movies, movie stars, and fashion, but nothing of substance. I would sometimes broach the subject by asking how she was feeling or if she ever felt sad or angry to have cancer. She would usually change the subject, and it became clear that she wasn't willing to talk about anything deeper. I didn't push. First of all, she wasn't the type of person you push. Second, I knew Toni was much closer to her than I would ever be, and I assumed she shared her deep thoughts with Toni.

I was constantly amazed at the positive spirit Joyce had. She nearly always had a smile on her face and laughed and giggled all the time. I rarely saw her without a smile.

One day I ran into her in the hallway of the inpatient cancer wing. She was walking with a doctor and chatting away, just like she always did. The doctor hugged her, and she came over to me and asked if I had met Chase, the boy in the room that we were walking by. I hadn't, so she offered to introduce me. I asked her how she knew him, and she explained that she knew most of the kids on the cancer floor and in the clinic.

Her doctor had asked her several years ago if she would be sort of a poster child for cancer. She was so positive and seemed to flow with all of the changes and stress that accompany cancer, and her doctor thought it would help families to meet an actual child with cancer and discover it was not necessarily a death sentence or something that had to ruin every part of a person's life. So whenever a new child was diagnosed, Joyce would meet them and reassure their family that it wasn't as bad as it might seem during the initial diagnosis. Her positive energy, her smile, and her hopefulness were contagious. She brought much hope to many families at our hospital.

One day I was sitting in the chaplains' office, resting after visiting several kids. Toni came into the office and asked if I would leave her alone for a few minutes. I could tell she was upset. I had never seen her upset or even shaken. She had an incredible sense of humor and could make jokes that would alleviate the pain of any situation. To see her visibly shaken was upsetting for me as well. I left the office and stayed away long after I was supposed to go home because I was too afraid to go back in and bother her.

Finally my pager went off, and the number displayed was the chaplains' office. I called it from the hallway phone.

Toni answered, trying to sound upbeat. "Hey, Leanne, I'm leaving. You can come and get your things now."

I walked into the office, expecting her to be gone, but she was still sitting at her desk, looking down. I couldn't tell if she had been crying and I didn't want to upset her, so I just sat there for a few minutes. Neither of us moved. Finally I broke the silence and asked, "You okay? Did something happen?"

She kept her gaze on her desk and simply said, "Joyce."

I knew something was terribly wrong. The silence in the room was audible.

After what seemed like an hour of complete silence, she said, "Joyce is tired. She's refusing more treatments. She has decided not to fight the cancer anymore."

I was confused. It had never seemed to me like Joyce struggled against her cancer. She always seemed so at peace with it and so certain about beating it. It had never dawned on me that it took energy to stay positive.

I was stunned and asked, "Will she die?"

"Yes," Toni whispered.

We didn't hear much from Joyce for several weeks. She and Toni would talk on the phone occasionally, but we didn't see her. Then we got the list of new admits, and Joyce was on it. I called Toni to tell her and then went to Joyce's room.

I was shocked when I walked in. It was the first time I had ever seen her in a hospital gown. She had no earrings, makeup, or scarves on her head. She was starting to bruise up and down her arms, a sign that the cancer was progressing and that she would not have long to live. She sat there not looking anything like the Hollywood starlets did in the movies, but she was her beautiful self! In fact, I had never really seen how lovely she was because her accessories and makeup covered her true looks. She was covered with bruises, had several IVs in her arms, and had only a few strands of hair on her head, and she was still lovely!

Her family was gathered around her bed. She introduced me and commented that she liked the boots I had on, but they would look better if they were mid-calf instead of knee-high. That was the fashion that season. She smiled, and I hugged her, promised to buy new boots, told her that Toni would be there soon, and prepared to leave the room.

Then Joyce asked me to pray for her. She told me that God had helped her decide not to receive treatments anymore. "God and I have been talking, and I told him how tired I am," she said. "And he told me that whenever I wanted, I could just let go and he would catch me—sort of like how children jump into a pool and are caught by their fathers. I want to do that. I want to let go. I want God to catch me and let me rest and not fight against this cancer anymore."

In reality, I wanted to pray that Joyce would change her mind and start treatments again, but I prayed as she had requested—that she would be able to let go and God would catch her in his loving arms. It was hard to make the words form in my mouth, and they stuck in my throat. I was relieved to say, "Amen." When I opened my eyes, Joyce still had hers shut and there was a smile on her face. I hugged her and left the room.

A few days later, Toni called me and, again trying to sound upbeat, said, "Hey, Leanne, I won't be in for a while today. I just got home. Joyce died early this morning, and I was there all night."

It was difficult to hear the sorrow in Toni's voice. I started to cry. I was sad that Joyce had died, that I hadn't been able to see her one last time, but mostly because I knew how heartbroken Toni was. I wanted to say something to make her feel better, but all I could think of was, "I have things under control here. Go to bed. I'll call you if I need anything." Then, through my tears, I added, "Was it a peaceful death?"

"Oh yeah," Toni said, sounding a bit better. "She died with that big old grin of hers on her face, and she told everyone who was gathered around her bed, 'Thank you for letting me go when I needed to. Thank you for letting me stop struggling. I'm tired and I need to rest. I want to be with God now and be free from all of this.'"

We stayed on the phone in silence for a few minutes. Toni finally broke the silence, saying, "You know, you're right. You have it under control. I might not come in. Thanks for understanding."

There wasn't much I could do or say to make Toni feel better. I couldn't do anything to make her sadness go away, but I did care and I'm glad she knew it.

Toni was invited to preach at Joyce's funeral. It was the first funeral for a child I had ever been to. I'd been to many funerals for adults and wasn't prepared for the sadness that is present when someone much too young dies and people gather together to try to find peace and comfort.

Toni stood up, and tears filled her eyes. She started talking about Joyce, and one by one the people around me began to wipe their tears as warm memories replaced the sorrow, at least for a few minutes. There were smiles and laughter as the journey of such a life-filled girl was recounted.

And then Toni read a passage from *The Velveteen Rabbit*:

"Real isn't how you are made," said the Skin Horse. "It's a thing that happens to you. When a child loves you for a long, long time, not just to play with, but REALLY loves you, then you become Real."

"Does it hurt?" asked the Rabbit.

"Sometimes," said the Skin Horse, for he was always truthful. "When you are Real you don't mind being hurt."

"Does it happen all at once, like being wound up," he asked, "or bit by bit?"

"It doesn't happen all at once," said the Skin Horse. "You become. It takes a long time. That's why it doesn't happen often to people who break easily, or have sharp edges, or who have to be carefully kept. Generally, by the time you are Real, most of your hair has been loved off, and your eyes drop out and you get loose in the joints and very shabby. But these things don't matter at all, because once you are Real you can't be ugly, except to people who don't understand."[1]

The Velveteen Rabbit is often studied as a book about our spiritual journey to become authentic people. For most people, the journey to become "real" takes a lifetime. For Joyce, it took twelve years, cancer, and knowing when it was time to let go and be with God.

1. Margery Williams Bianco, *The Velveteen Rabbit* (Philadelphia: Doubleday & Company, 1922), 14–15.

10

Tony

One of the duties of being a chaplain was being on call at night. The reason for a call in the middle of the night could be something very dramatic, such as a child dying or a child being brought in from a car accident, or it could be for a less dramatic reason such as a parent feeling overwhelmed and scared in the middle of the night and asking to speak to a chaplain. Usually, though, a page meant that something serious had happened. Some of the most difficult situations I ever faced began with a call from my pager.

Accidents happen, and they are heartbreaking. Accidental shootings, drownings, and car wrecks were always difficult calls to respond to, and they often meant staying up all night. The chaplains had to minister not only to the families but also to the staff, who never got used to seeing children hurt and in pain, even though these things happened regularly. Compassion was always part of the job. The reality for everyone at the hospital was that we were working with children, and that meant never becoming totally detached.

By far, the worst on-call situations involved abused children. Often, if I got called, it was a life-or-death situation. These unfortunate little ones would come in with multiple broken bones or internal injuries, having been burned with cigarettes, beaten, bruised, or molested. These kids' situations were the most heartbreaking ones we ever dealt with. They were wounded because of the deliberate action of an adult. There was no reason that the child being brought in should be in pain or die.

The staff was particularly affected by these children. The worst part for them was that until the child protective services arrived, did interviews, and could prove which adult had harmed the child, the parents were present. And they were needed. A child, even if he or she has been abused, loves those parents and needs them nearby for comfort, and the staff needs the parents to sign admittance papers and give the child's medical history.

The tension was often so thick between the staff and the parents that chaplains were expected to act as a buffer between them. I must admit, it was hard for me to be kind as well. I tried to remind myself that a person who would hurt a child had most likely been terribly abused as a child too and was continuing a family pattern they didn't begin. I would also remind myself that we didn't know for certain who had hurt the child, and it wasn't my place to judge. I would tell myself these things, place a fake smile on my face, and try my best to be compassionate and kind to people I wanted to scream at and have removed from the hospital!

One night my pager went off. I called the operator and was forwarded to the emergency room. A child being transported via ambulance was suspected of being abused. His mother, Mary, had come home from work and found blood on his pillow, which she discovered was coming out of one of his ears. She also noticed that he had a black eye, and she could not get him to wake up. Her boyfriend had been babysitting him while she was at work, and his story was that the boy had fallen off a chair in the kitchen but was fine when he put him to bed.

The police and social services had been called, and they needed a chaplain to be at the emergency room when the mom arrived. The child was nonresponsive and barely breathing, and serious head trauma was suspected.

I dressed as quickly as I could and got to the emergency room just moments before Mary, her mother, Alice, and Mary's three friends arrived. They were all talking at once, crying and yelling; two of the friends were intoxicated. I took them into a small, private family waiting room and introduced myself.

Mary was quiet and clearly in shock. She had returned from work and found her child barely alive. Had she not gone into his room and checked on him, he surely would have died.

Her friends were very animated, and it was difficult to tell which part of their dramatic selves was because of the injury and which was because of the alcohol. They were shouting that the boyfriend, Terrance, should not be allowed into the hospital because he had hurt this child. They wanted him to be arrested and to go to prison for what he'd done.

I asked Mary what she wanted. She just sat there, numb and without any expression on her face, tears flowing down her cheeks. Alice, the grandmother of the child, asked to speak to me privately. We went into another small room, and she began telling me she had feared something like this would happen. Terrance had a history of violence. He had a prison record and had hit her daughter on several occasions. He also hated the child, Tony, because he felt like her daughter gave all her attention to the child and not to him. She was certain he had hurt Tony, but of course since there were no witnesses, there was no way to prove it yet.

I appreciated hearing from Alice and went back into the room where Mary was. She was still unwilling to speak. I went into the trauma room to see what was going on with Tony. He was a tiny little guy. They had stripped him down and were doing life support on him. His heart had quit beating several times, and they were trying to keep him alive until the medications that he'd been given to reduce the brain swelling could take effect.

This was clearly a badly hurt child. By now the black eye his mother had reported covered half his face. His eye was swollen shut, and bruises had appeared all over his body. He hadn't fallen off a chair; he had been beaten.

I went back into the waiting room and gave Mary a report as honestly and yet as hopefully as I could. "It appears your son has been beaten. They're doing all they can to keep him alive until the medicines can work," I said. She just sat there crying.

The nurse came in and said that there was a man at the admittance desk named Terrance asking to see Mary. She suddenly woke up as if she had been pricked with a pin, and using all kinds of expletives, she screamed that in no way was he ever to come near her or her son again. She asked the police to kick him out. One of her drunk friends tried to leave the room and beat him up, but her other friend stopped her. I decided to go get coffee for everyone and try to sober up the group of friends.

On the way to the coffeepot, I stopped by the room where the staff was working with Tony. He had stabilized a bit, and they were taking him for a head X-ray and then up to the intensive care unit. The staff was exhausted and clearly upset. I told them that it was most likely the boyfriend who had injured the child and that the mom had refused him entrance, so they wouldn't have to see or deal with him.

Mary was clearly also a victim in this situation. She had trusted Terrance, or else she would have never left her son with him. Her grief was quite genuine, and she was clearly very upset that her child had been hurt. But the staff wanted little to do with her. It might have been because they felt she should have known better than to leave the child with her boyfriend, or it might have been because they were tired and upset over the entire situation and simply did not have the emotional energy to speak with this upset mother. That was my job!

I took Mary and Alice up to the ER waiting room and convinced Mary's friends that they needed to go home and regroup so they could support her in the coming days. Mary, Alice, and I spent the next three hours talking about how they were feeling and about Tony. They told me stories about his birth, how smart he was, and funny things he did and said, and then something would trigger their tears.

I listened to their stories and then periodically went into the unit to check on Tony. It took a long time for him to return from X-ray, and the report was not good. He had suffered severe head trauma and had terrible swelling. They had to cut a hole in his scalp to try to reduce pressure, but even that wasn't working well. His head was simply swelling too fast to control. I reported this to Mary and Alice, and I felt sorry for Tony's mom, who was clearly frightened and guilt ridden.

After a few hours, Tony was stabilized. I asked Mary and Alice if they would like to visit him. I described to them all of his wounds and told them what to expect as they entered his room. His head was bandaged, and there were all kinds of tubes and monitors hooked up to him.

We entered the unit, and Mary almost collapsed. Her legs were shaking so badly, they could barely carry her into his room. Alice and I were on both sides of her, holding her up. When we entered the room, Alice took one look at Tony and ran out. His mother practically laid herself on top of him. It was hard to tell if she was trying to hold him or trying to be held by him.

She placed her face by his ear and kept whispering, "Mommy is here. Mommy is here. I won't let anyone hurt you ever again! Mommy is here!" She was in such pain that I couldn't help my own tears.

The nurse came in and asked Tony's mom if she had any questions. She asked about some of the bags hanging from the IV pole, and the nurse explained the antiswelling medication. "Will my son wake up soon?" Mary wondered out loud.

The nurse replied with as much compassion as she could muster, "I hope he will. We all hope he will, but he is badly hurt. Do you understand?"

Mary nodded that she did.

The nurse continued. "It's been a long night. You and your mom should get some sleep. If he wakes up, I'll personally come and get you so you can see him."

I walked with Mary back to the waiting room and found Alice sitting on the couch. I could tell that they were both exhausted and said, "You should really try and get some sleep. If Tony does wake up, he'll need you, so while he's sleeping, you should be as well."

I found blankets and pillows for them, and they both lay down. I had also started to feel tired. The adrenaline had worn off, and I wanted to sleep myself. I told them I was going home but would check with them as soon I got in the next day.

I had to go to the chaplains' office and fill out a report so that the other chaplains would know what had happened during the night. I also called the ICU nurse and asked her to page me if anything happened during the rest of the night.

I drove home and got there at 4:00 a.m. I slept for a few hours but had little Tony and his mom on my mind, so I decided to go back to the hospital. After a shower, which soothed my exhausted body and soul, I ate breakfast and finally arrived at the hospital about 8:30 a.m. I went straight to the intensive care unit to check on Tony, and on my way I peeked into the waiting room where I had left his mother and grandmother sleeping. The couch where Alice had been was empty. There was no sign of a blanket or anything else.

Mary was still sleeping on her couch. I walked closer to see if she was awake, and to my horror, there was a man lying with her under the blanket. Surely this was not her boyfriend! Surely she hadn't let him into the hospital.

My presence must have awakened them. She looked up and said, "Oh, hi!"

"Hi," I said. "I couldn't sleep, so I came in to check on Tony. Have you heard anything?"

"Oh yes, he's waking up a little. I got to talk to him once earlier this morning."

"Do they seem hopeful?" I asked.

"I can't tell. Could you go and check?"

I didn't ask who the man sleeping on the couch was. I didn't want to know. I went into the unit and asked the nurse what was going on with Tony.

Her response was hostile. "He's very badly hurt and will most likely die. And his mother is out there kissing and sleeping with the man who did this to him!"

I felt sick. I had assumed the man on the couch was Terrance, but denial had stopped me from accepting the truth. I went in to Tony's room and found him semiconscious. For the first time I could see that his eyes were green, though I could see only one of them since the other was so badly swollen. He was calm, clearly too injured to move. His arms and legs had been bandaged to stabilize the broken bones. He was still too unstable to place real casts on yet. I stood beside him looking into his good eye and wondering how anyone could ever be angry or out of control enough to do this much harm to a five-year-old precious little boy.

I went back to the waiting room, and Mary was now sitting on Terrance's lap. I was furious as I walked up to her.

"Tony is very sick," I told her, "and they're still not sure if he'll make it."

"Can we go back and see him?" she asked.

I wanted to slap her. I feel bad saying that, but it's true. I was incensed that she would even ask if the man who had hurt her little boy could see him! I wondered where social services were in all of this. I didn't know what to say, so I said I would check with his nurse.

The nurse's reaction was even more extreme than mine. She cried at the suggestion that this man would ever be allowed touch the child again, but she acknowledged that Tony's mother had the right to let whomever she wanted visit the child. We could not legally stop her.

I went back to Mary. She was still sitting on Terrance's lap, and he was stroking her hair and comforting her.

"He can visit," I said, "but to be honest, we don't want anyone who might upset Tony visiting. It wouldn't be good for him to get upset."

She listened carefully and then stood up, took Terrance by the hand, and led him into the room. We entered Tony's room, and he smiled at his mother. She went to one side of the bed and Terrance to the other. I stayed close to Terrance just to let him know he wasn't to do anything to upset this child.

Mary smiled and spoke lovingly to Tony. Terrance spoke as well. "Hey, little guy. It's me, Terrance, your buddy. I can't wait for you to get out of this place. You hang in there."

I was shaking from watching this man act like he had nothing to do with all of this. I took deep breaths to keep myself from saying anything.

All of a sudden Tony tried to speak. He looked at Terrance and moved his lips. Mary moved close and asked him to say it again because we couldn't understand him. Tony again said something to Terrance.

This time Terrance turned white and fell to his knees beside the bed. He began to sob and said, "Did you hear what he said? He told me that God forgives me and he forgives me. . . . He told me that God forgives me and he forgives me."

I wasn't looking at Tony. I was looking at Terrance, crumpled and weeping on his knees beside the bed. It almost looked like he was praying at an altar.

Mary spoke to Tony again, then said, "He's trying to say something else."

I looked at his little lips, and he said, "I'm going now. God wants me."

I called the nurse. A monitor went off, and several nurses came running. I tried to pick Terrance up off the floor, but it took a male nurse to finally get him to stand. They rushed us out of the room so they could resuscitate Tony, whose heart had once again failed.

They worked on him for at least an hour, maybe longer. Time was blurred. Tony's heart would start and stop and start again. Finally the staff admitted he was too injured to save. The brain swelling and internal injuries were just too much for his little body to fight any longer.

I never saw Tony's mother or Terrance again, but I did hear that Terrance was sent to prison as a result of causing Tony's death. I have no idea how long he served or where he is now. But I have never forgotten this child who was so badly hurt and yet spoke words of God's forgiveness to the man who caused his death. And in those times when I have been wronged and find forgiveness impossible, I remember a five-year-old who did the impossible.

11

The Cystic Fibrosis Gang

While I worked as a chaplain, I also held a part-time job as the youth director at a nearby church, so I spent time with the teens in the cystic fibrosis unit and with the teens at my church. I assumed that the teens at the church, who for the most part had blessed lives with good health, nice families, and bright futures, would be happier and more hopeful than the teens at the hospital, who struggled daily with a disease that had no mercy on them. I was wrong.

The kids at the hospital were amazingly upbeat, full of life, and hopeful. I'm not sure what the cause of that was. Perhaps it was because they didn't expect to live long, so they were determined to live life to the fullest as long as they could. Perhaps it was because they would hear reports of medical progress and breakthroughs for cystic fibrosis on a regular basis and believed that it would be cured in their lifetime.

Perhaps they were good at denial and pushing their fears and anxieties into the back corners of their minds. Or perhaps they were simply teens who, just like the teens at my church, feared nothing and lived for the day at hand.

For whatever reason, I always marveled at the fact that the teens at the church and those at the hospital were so similar. They were all full of life, talkative, having relationship drama, laughing one minute and crying the next, worrying about their appearance, and doing all the things teens do.

I called the cystic fibrosis kids the "gang" because I rarely found one of them alone no matter what time of day or night day it was. They treated the cystic fibrosis unit as their own personal clubhouse. They watched television together, played Ping-Pong in the lounge, and sat in each other's rooms and on each other's beds, talking, laughing, and, as all teens do, flirting with one another.

They hated hospital food, so they were given all kinds of regular food that they could cook for themselves in the microwave. The nurses were constantly hanging up signs telling them to clean up their mess in the kitchen area, which they ignored in normal teenage fashion. Everyone on the staff would spend a lot of time telling them to go to bed, asking them to stop chatting after ten in the evening, and grumbling about their messes.

Despite all the complaining by staff, the kids were absolutely adored. I couldn't help but love them extra for being regular teens with such irregular lives. Their courage, their refusal to let their disease stop them from being joyful, and their ability to push on even when they were so sick impressed me greatly.

The only time I could ever determine the toll the disease had on them was when one of the gang would die. These teens knew death was a possibility, and while the doctors worked hard to do all they could to extend their lives, every year one or two of them would die.

———

I remember the first time I was called to the unit because one of the teens was very ill. I walked in expecting to see the gang playing Ping-Pong, to smell pizza cooking in the microwave, and to hear their music blasting over the sound of the television in the lounge. Instead, it was quiet. Several kids were in their room with their doors shut—alone. Some were sitting together in their rooms, whispering. None were smiling or laughing.

I went into the room of two of the teens I knew well. They asked me if I knew Julie was very sick. I told them I had come to visit her but thought I would check on them as well. They began telling me in detail what had happened and why and how a person dies from cystic fibrosis. They sounded not like the teens from my church but more like doctors with specialties in cystic fibrosis. They used medical jargon and no longer spoke with Valley girl accents. And they were no longer animated teens—they were all business. It was during times like these I realized just how brave and strong these kids were.

I was glad to be given the detailed update on Julie. I walked down the hall to peek into her room, which was filled with people. I hadn't met her before, but I guessed that the two people standing closest to her bed were her parents. It's not difficult to figure out who the parents are. Their grief over facing the death of their child is obviously more intense than anyone else's in the room.

There were also some older people who I guessed were grandparents, and then there were several nurses. Some were working the shift, and others had come in because she was so ill and they wanted to see her one last time. The medical technicians who had drawn her blood daily, the respiratory therapists, the social workers, and even the woman who ran the gift shop were there around her bed.

My supervisor, Toni, who had known Julie since she was a small child, was standing in the middle of the room, not saying anything but bringing comfort to the group simply by her nonanxious spirit. She was rubbing shoulders, handing out Kleenex, and sort of rocking back and forth from her heels to her toes. Watching her reminded me of a mother soothing her baby by wiping the child's tears and gently rocking them back to sleep.

I didn't stay long. There were so many people in the room that I wasn't needed, so I decided to go to each room and check on the other teens. Most were quiet. They didn't share their feelings but again spoke scientifically about the disease. Many said they were glad they were not showing the signs of complications that the dying teen had shown.

It seemed each one was assessing where they were in the course of the disease and trying to figure out when it would overtake them. No one said it, but I could sense the truth as they spoke. It was obvious—less in their words and more in their tone of voice—that as much as they tried to act like life was normal for them, they had a giant to face every day, and when one of them was losing the battle, the giant grew taller and more intimidating.

As I listened to them, I kept picturing them as David, who had volunteered to bravely face the giant Goliath. I recalled the story where he walked toward the place where he would meet Goliath, stopping to pick up five stones to use in his slingshot. I imagined how small he was next to the giant when he came face-to-face with him, and I pictured each of these children standing face-to-face with their own giant. I remembered how David said that though Goliath was strong and had powerful weapons, he, David, would win the battle because he had God on his side. I hoped and prayed that these teens had God to lean on and that he would soon slay the giants they faced.

After visiting all of the teens, I walked back to Julie's room and once again peeked in. Some of the nurses and staff had left, but Toni and Julie's parents and relatives were still there. Julie's mother was now seated next to her and resting her head on the bed. I wasn't sure if she was sleeping or praying. Maybe she was doing both. I didn't introduce myself or say anything. I did pray, though—a prayer of strength and courage for all who had gathered in Julie's room.

The next day Toni called to tell me that she wasn't coming in. "Hey, Leanne, I am wiped out. I was with Julie and her family all night. She really hung on, but she died peacefully early this morning."

"Yeah," I replied, "I heard she had died. You sound exhausted. Can you go to bed?"

"I want to, but someone needs to check on the kids in the unit. When we knew Julie was about to die, we woke some of them and they were able to say goodbye, but I'm sure they're a mess. Do you have time to check on them?"

"Of course I do!" I said. "I'll go there first thing, okay? You sleep. I promise to check on them."

I knew the teens would have complex feelings about the death of their friend. They would have the grief we all have over losing a friend, but they would also have renewed fear about their own mortality and uncertainty about their future. One thing I knew about teens is that while drama is a huge part of their lives, when things get intense they tend to shut down. Perhaps it's too frightening to start letting their emotions out. They're afraid that if they start to cry, they may never stop. And some feel embarrassed to shed tears or show emotion in front of others. They don't want others to see them get upset. Some girls even fear looking ugly if they cry, and the last thing any teen girl wants is to look ugly!

In the cystic fibrosis unit, there was another reason the teens wouldn't share negative emotions: they were protective of one another. They worked hard at being hopeful, upbeat, and positive for each other. They didn't want to say or do anything that might upset someone in their group.

I knew the teens needed to express their true feelings after the death of their friend, but I also knew they would need help getting started. As I left for the unit, I stopped by my car and grabbed a box of markers and some paper. When I arrived, I found most of the teens—seven of them—sitting in a circle and talking quietly. They looked rather stunned and in shock. I asked if I could join them. I placed the paper and markers in the center of the circle and invited them to draw if they wanted to. I explained that they needed to get their feelings out, and sometimes drawing could be an easier way to express them than using words.

They sat there for a long time, silent and not doing much. Finally one of them took a sheet of paper and some markers and started to draw. That was all it took to motivate the others to do the same. In a matter of about five minutes, they were all drawing. It was quiet, and all I could hear was the sound of markers on paper. They drew for what felt like a long time. I tried not to look at their pictures so they could have privacy.

After they finished drawing, I suggested that everyone lay their pictures down in the middle of the circle so that we could all see them, and then if anyone felt comfortable sharing, they could. One by one they laid their pictures in the center. They were more colorful than I had expected, but what I noticed immediately was that three of them looked quite similar. In fact, they were almost identical.

They began sharing their pictures with one another. One teen had drawn a series of question marks in all shapes and sizes. They were different colors and turned every which way on the page. "This is how I feel inside," he said. "I have so many questions. Why did Julie die now, and why do some of the kids with CF die sooner than others? I don't get it. I mean, I have CF and my sister doesn't. I'm glad she doesn't have it, but why do I? It's unfair, and now I'm wondering when I'll die. How do we know when it will be our time?"

Another teen had drawn a cross with Christ hanging on it. Then she'd taken a black marker and scribbled all over the picture. "Here's my picture. I hope I don't upset anyone. I used to love Jesus . . . I used to trust God, but now I've seen so many sad things. I've had so many friends die. I don't even know if there is a God anymore. I've prayed so many prayers. I prayed for Julie all night long, asking God to heal her. I'm just sick of it. I'm sick of begging and nothing happening. So I scribbled Jesus out. I'm sorry if anyone feels upset about it, but we're supposed to draw how we really feel, right?"

I nodded.

Then a third teen shared her picture. It was one of the three that looked similar, and in it a girl was surrounded by a bright light and standing on top of a small green hill. She was smiling and looked content. As she shared her picture, the teen began to blush and said, "I know this might sound weird, but I had a dream last night, and I saw Julie. She didn't say anything, but I think she appeared to me to let me know she was all right. She looked so happy and the light around her was so bright, and the grass was the greenest color I have ever seen. This marker isn't even the right color! It was so much greener. I'm not sure, but I'm pretty sure she was in heaven."

The look of shock that came over two of the other teens' faces would have been funny if it had not been such a sad time. At nearly the same exact moment, the color began to drain from their faces and their mouths dropped open. One of them said, "I can't believe this. See my picture?" We all looked at her picture, and it was also of a girl in the midst of a bright yellow light and standing on a green hill. "I had a dream last night too! And this is what I saw. It's the same as yours! Do you think Julie appeared to us both? Did we see heaven?"

No one spoke. A stunned silence filled the room. I was covered with goose bumps. Finally one of the teens broke the silence by asking the person who had drawn the third similar picture if she had had a dream as well.

The teen looked extremely embarrassed and said, "No. I couldn't sleep because I was so upset. And for some reason I felt afraid that if I let myself go to sleep, I wouldn't wake up again. I felt like if I went to sleep I would die. So I wasn't sleeping."

Another teen asked how she knew what the dreams were if she wasn't asleep. She was quiet for about two minutes and then said, "I saw her, but I was awake. She . . ." There was a long pause. "She appeared to me, like a ghost, only not scary. I was sitting up in my bed trying to read my book, but it was hard because I couldn't really concentrate. I heard a noise, and when I looked up, there she was. You would think I would have been afraid, but she was so beautiful and there was this calm feeling in the room. I sat there looking at her for a long time. We didn't speak with words, but somehow she told me that I wouldn't die if I went to sleep, so I should lie down and go to sleep. I lay down, and when I looked up, she was gone."

One of the teens asked the others, "So does this mean Julie is okay? Does this mean she's in heaven?" Everyone started talking animatedly, assuring him that the dreams and the vision were proof that Julie was fine.

The atmosphere in the room shifted from the place of sorrow I had entered to an atmosphere found at a high school ball game. The teens laughed and chatted, and then someone decided it was time to eat. Life had returned to normal. The music came back on, and the microwave hum was once again a constant background noise.

I began to gather up the pictures because I wanted to save them. As I picked up the picture of Christ on the cross, the girl who had drawn it came over to me and asked if she could take it and if she could borrow the markers. She sat down at a table, turned the picture over, and once again drew Christ hanging on the cross. Only this time, his cross was placed on a green hill and had light shining all around it. It looked very much like the pictures of Julie the others had drawn, but instead of Julie standing on the hill surrounded by light, it was Jesus.

"I want to hang this picture in my room," she said. "When I drew it, I was questioning whether or not God was with me anymore, but now I know! God is with us, isn't he? God is with all of us no matter what." And then she looked up and whispered, "Thank you, Julie!"

12

Jessica

Our hospital served children of all ages. As a chaplain, I spent much time in the neonatal intensive care unit of the children's hospital, where premature infants who were born at adult hospitals would be transported for specialized care. These babies were so tiny. They were often less than two pounds and were laid in isolated beds where they could be kept warm and monitored. I loved that unit and would often go into it to hold the babies and watch them grow.

Chaplains were called to that unit often because babies with severe prematurity would sometimes die. I spent many nights sitting with parents and helping them through what would be the most painful experience of their lives as they watched their baby die, along with all the hopes and dreams they had for that child.

As intensely sad as the death of an infant is, the joy when a very sick infant makes it through a life-threatening situation is equally powerful. I would always be amazed at how quickly the staff, myself included, could bond with a baby who did nothing but lie in their bed. I suppose it might have been because human beings have an inborn, biological urge to see our species live. The continuation of life depends on babies surviving. I think, though, more than any biological urge, the instant bonding was because the parents wanted their baby to survive, and through sheer empathy, the staff would bond quickly with this new baby that the parents clearly loved so much. I could not meet one of these brokenhearted parents and not immediately feel their deep pain. On the other hand, the relief and joy they felt when their baby improved was a feeling like no other. You could feel their pain and share their joy!

Jessica had been one of these infants in our neonatal intensive care unit. She had been born a few years before I began my work as a chaplain, and I met her on a day when I was visiting the neonatal intensive care unit. I had scrubbed my hands and put on a gown and was checking on one of the babies who had come in a few days earlier. I was happy to learn that he was doing well and was expected to make it. He just needed what the nurses called "fattening up."

While I was speaking to the nurse caring for this little one, one of the other nurses came up to us, apologized for interrupting, and said that Jessica had come by for a visit. I had no idea who Jessica was, but from the excitement in the unit, I assumed she was one of the sick babies who had survived and gone home. It was common for their parents to bring them back and show them off to the staff, who had grown to love these little ones as if they were their aunts, uncles, or grandparents.

The nurse excused herself and with a huge smile scurried off to see Jessica. I checked on several other babies and overheard lots of buzz about Jessica. One nurse told me that this child had been one of the sickest babies the staff had ever cared for and that she had been in the unit for several months before she was able to go home. The nurse said how sweet Jessica's mother and father were and that they had never left her side the entire time she was in the unit. As the nurses took turns leaving and returning to the unit, it was obvious that this child was special—extra special—to many of them.

I walked out of the unit into the hallway and saw a woman standing beside a stroller. I assumed this was Jessica's mother, because it was rare to have a stroller in this part of the hospital. I went over to her and asked if she was Jessica's mom. She smiled and introduced herself as Jenny. I told her that I had never seen the staff so excited by a visit of a "graduate" from the neonatal unit as I had when she and Jessica arrived.

I peeked into the stroller and saw a beautiful baby with huge blue eyes and tiny lips. Her head was too big for her body and was covered in the thickest, waviest blonde hair I'd ever seen on a child. Her eyelashes were also very long. I had never seen anything like them, even on supermodels who wear false ones. She didn't look like a baby, but rather like a doll that you would buy at the store. I told Jenny that Jessica was the most beautiful baby I had ever seen.

Jenny beamed with pride and said, "She really is pretty, isn't she? It's part of the syndrome." She explained that her daughter had been born with a rare form of dwarfism, which is characterized by tiny bones and a regular-sized head. Since the bones are so small, the head appears large, even though it is normal size. Babies with this syndrome are born with a full head of hair and lovely eyelashes. Most babies die shortly after birth, and there has been little study on the long-term life expectancy because it's a very rare condition and so few of them survive the first few days of life.

Jessica had been expected to die shortly after birth but had surprised everyone by living. In fact, she was now three years old. She could not sit up unless her head was supported, but she was talking and was very bright. It took me a few minutes to adjust to the reality that this baby was actually a three-year-old.

I squatted down to look in the stroller again and spoke to Jessica. Sure enough, she responded. Except for her tiny frame, she was a normal three-year-old eating her snack and asking her mommy to go home. She was darling. I could see how the staff had come to love her so much.

Her mother and I talked a few more moments, then I went on to visit others in the older children's units. I waved goodbye to Jessica, and she blew me a kiss.

Nearly a year later, I heard from the neonatal ICU nurses that Jessica had been admitted to the hospital. She was scheduled for surgery on her heart. Her mother had shared with me the external symptoms of her dwarfism, but I soon learned she had internal issues as well. One of them was a heart valve in need of repair.

When I stopped by Jessica's room, I was again struck by her beauty. Her little body had not grown much, but her hair was longer and her eyes were just as huge as I remembered. Her mother, to my surprise, remembered me, and we began to chat. I was struck by how calm Jenny seemed, and I asked her if she was having any anxiety about the surgery. She told me the doctors had assured her it was a common surgery, and while things could always go wrong, they were not worried about it at all.

Jessica was sitting up on her bed, propped up with pillows supporting her head, and playing with a tiny glass tea set.

"Hi," I said, "I love your tea set. It's so pretty! It looks like it's very special."

"It is," she said, clearly pleased that I liked it. "My grandmother bought it for me. It was a present because I had to come back to the hospital."

I watched as she carefully arranged the teacups and saucers she had set out until, in her opinion, they were right where they belonged. She looked up and sheepishly said, "I'd give you some, but I only have enough for us."

"Who is 'us'?" I asked.

"My friends," she replied, pointing to each cup. "One for Taggy and one for Toad."

I felt honored that I had been introduced to her imaginary friends!

Jenny told me that Jessica had had these friends from the time she had started to talk and that their names still made her laugh. Jessica would greet her friends each morning and make sure they were tucked into bed with her each night. She took Taggy and Toad with her wherever she went. Jenny laughed as she told me she was glad Jessica had imaginary friends to take along instead of a blanket or doll that could be left behind or lost. "We can never lose Taggy and Toad!" she said.

I watched as Jessica poured tea for her friends and laughed and talked to them. It was delightful to see her so content. I wondered what Taggy and Toad looked like. Were they children or adults? Were they people or animals? Was Toad a frog? I asked Jessica what they looked like. She simply looked at me and said, "Look at them, silly. They look like this," and she pointed to the empty places next to the teacups.

Her surgery was scheduled for the next morning, and I offered to come and sit with the family. Jenny told me that her husband and mother would be with her, but she would love for me to come by and meet them. She didn't need me to stay with her the entire time.

The next morning I arrived extra early because I knew the surgery was happening first thing. Jessica's family members were the only ones in the waiting room. They all had cups of coffee and were quietly talking. As soon as I approached, Jenny introduced me. I told her mother how much fun I'd had watching Jessica play tea with her imaginary friends. She was thrilled her granddaughter had enjoyed the tea set so much.

I wondered if the family had heard anything yet, and they said that only a few minutes before I arrived, the surgical nurse had come out to say that everything was going well. The nurse thought Jessica would be out of surgery within the half hour. I asked if they needed anything, and they said they were fine. I promised to stop by the recovery room later and left.

As I walked down the hall, my pager went off. I found a phone and called the hospital operator, who told me to go immediately to surgery. My heart skipped a beat. I could tell from the operator's voice that something was urgent, and I hoped it wasn't anything to do with Jessica.

I walked—or rather, ran—into the surgery area. A nurse was waiting there for me.

"Are you the chaplain?" she barked, clearly in panic mode.

"Yeah, I am. What can I do for you?"

She took a deep breath and said, "We have a little girl in heart surgery. Her heart has stopped twice, and they're having a hard time stabilizing her. I just don't know if she'll make it. Can you sit with her parents?"

I could not believe my ears. I had just spoken to her parents, and they had heard that everything was going well. I asked the name of the child, hoping it would not be Jessica. It was.

"I know the parents," I said, trying to catch my breath. "I'll be here. Any update you can give us will be great."

I walked back into the surgery waiting room. There were two other sets of parents there, and I asked Jessica's family to come with me to a more private area. They probably could tell from the look of shock on my face that something wasn't right. They were completely silent as they gathered their things and followed me into a private room. I told them I had been called and there was some kind of problem with the surgery. I knew I wasn't supposed to tell them how serious it was. That was the job of the doctor or nurse. I said someone would be out shortly to update them.

We sat in complete silence for what seemed like an hour. I peeked at my watch, and in reality, only seven minutes had passed by the time the surgical nurse came into the room. She told the parents that Jessica's heart had started to beat irregularly and that the situation was very serious. The doctors were doing everything they could to help her, but she had also had a seizure, so they were having a difficult time regulating her heart.

Jessica's mother spoke. Her voice was quiet and shaky, and I could tell that she had to force her breath through her tense vocal cords. She asked, "So Jessica might die?"

The nurse hesitated and then said, "We are not God. I can't tell you if she's going to die, but I have to be honest—it is a possibility."

Jenny buried her head in her hands, and her husband and mother moved closer to comfort her. The nurse told them that she had to get back into surgery but would keep us informed. I promised to stay with the family.

Jenny suddenly sat straight up and said, "No! I want you to be with her. I want God to be with her. If she dies, I want someone holy with her. And she needs to be baptized. Will you go be with her and baptize her?"

I was in shock and sat there stunned. I was clearly not God. I didn't know what to say.

The nurse stood up and said, "Yes, she can!" She walked out of the room and told me to follow.

I turned to Jenny, squeezed her hands, and said, "I will be with Jessica." And then I said, "Thank you." I don't know why I said that. It might have been because I was grateful someone had taken my role as chaplain seriously. Or it might have been because I was so honored to be trusted with such precious tasks as being with her child and baptizing her.

Tears filled her eyes, and she said, "No, thank *you*!"

The nurse was clearly growing impatient because she needed to get back into surgery. I hugged Jenny and followed the nurse through the wide metal doors with a huge sign that read "Do Not Enter." Just inside of those doors was the scrub room. The nurse hurriedly washed her hands and showed me how to wash mine. I thought I already knew how because I had scrubbed up so many times as I entered the neonatal ICU, but this was much more intense. I scrubbed up to my elbows and was cautioned not to touch anything. I was given a gown and small cap for my hair and booties to cover my shoes with. Then we scrubbed a second time and put on rubber gloves.

There was a small door separating us from the actual surgery. The nurse left me in the scrub room and went into the surgical area. I wondered if the surgeon would really let me enter.

The nurse returned and had a grim look on her face. "What do you need for the baptism?" she asked.

"A cup of water," I said.

She opened a sterile cup, unscrewed the top, and handed it to me. "We need to do this quickly. They'll get angry if you get in the way."

I was officially scared now. I had never done a baptism before and was intimidated by the idea that the staff might get angry with me if I didn't do it fast enough.

As soon as we entered the room, I paused to bless the water, staying away from the bed. I saw Jessica lying so tiny on the huge operating table. I could only see her face. Everything else was covered, and people were on every side of her, furiously working.

The surgeon looked up and said, "You can come to this end." He pointed to the end of the bed where her head was. "Will that work for you?"

I nodded and went to the end of the bed. I closed my eyes and said a short prayer, asking God to work a miracle once again in this little girl's life. Then I dipped my fingers in the plastic cup and sprinkled her head while I said, "Jessica, I baptize you in the name of the Father, Son, and Holy Spirit." The surgeon and several nurses crossed themselves after I finished.

The nurse pulled me over to the far side of the operating room, and I stayed there for the next fifteen minutes. I couldn't see much. I didn't want to see much! I could tell that things were not going well. They were shouting orders and sighing, and their frustration was obvious.

Finally the movement in the room stopped. The surgeon said nothing as he walked out. The nurses began disconnecting machines. Jessica had died.

The surgical nurse and I took off our gowns and gloves and walked back to tell the family what had happened. They knew from the looks on our faces that the news was not good. The nurse explained that the doctor would be out shortly to answer their questions. He arrived only a few moments later and was clearly shaken up. Very professionally he explained to them in scientific terms what had happened. I don't remember them asking him any questions. He explained that they would be able to see Jessica and spend time with her body after she was cleaned up.

I sat with them for about an hour until a nurse came and invited them to see their child. Jessica's family bravely walked into her room. The nurses had dressed her in a fresh gown and brushed her hair. She was lying on her back with her eyes closed and her hands folded on her tummy. She looked like an angel.

Her parents spent time with her, and then Jenny asked if she could speak to me privately. Everyone left the room, and the two of us stood next to each other facing Jessica.

Jenny turned to me and quietly said, "I was never a religious person until Jessica was born. But when she was born so sick and then lived, I knew God had done a miracle. I began to pray, and I thanked God for her every day!

"You know her imaginary friends? They were so real to her. She spoke to them and played with them every day. I always thought they were just fun—a thing little children do. I mean, lots of my friends have kids who play with their imaginary friends. But yesterday when Jessica was playing, she told me her friends wanted her to come with them. I asked her where they wanted her to come, and she said, 'Heaven.' I don't want you to think I'm crazy, but do you think her friends might have been angels? Do you think that maybe

God sent them to play with her so that when she died, she wouldn't be afraid?" She broke into tears, fell to her knees, and kissed Jessica's tiny hand.

I never answered her questions. I wasn't sure who Taggy and Toad really were. But ever since that day, when children introduce me to their imaginary friends, I remember little Jessica and can't help but wonder if perhaps angels are closer than we realize.

13

Polly

Polly wasn't a child. She was twenty-one years old when I first met her, on the day I was born. She was my mother, and I was her second child. My mother wasn't perfect, but she loved her four children deeply. She had graduated high school, met my father, and married him three months later. He began seminary, and she followed him from church to church his entire career, staying home and caring for her four children.

My parents had planned for Mom to go to college after my dad finished seminary, but once we kids came along, she never had the time or energy to return. Finally, when her last child entered high school, she decided it was time to go back to school. She had always wanted to become a nurse, and she began studying math and preparing for her entrance exams. She was excited and ready. We were all proud of her.

As it turned out, Mom was not able to even start her degree. There was a problem: she had a foot that didn't work right.

Sometimes it would feel numb, and other times it would drag as she tried to lift it. It didn't hurt or worry her, but it was an inconvenience.

One day we went to an amusement park, and after several hours of walking, Mom started to cry. I asked her what was wrong, and she said that her foot had started worrying her. To be honest, I was a little irritated with her for ruining our time by crying, and I made a little joke, saying, "Well, Mom, I don't think you need to cry. No one ever died of a foot that wouldn't work."

I regret saying that more than anything I have ever said, because you can die from a foot that won't work. My mother did.

It took nearly a year to find out what was wrong. Mom went to several doctors who had differing opinions of what might be the problem with her foot. One told her it could be a pinched nerve and sent her to physical therapy. It didn't help. Another asked her if she was happily married or if she was using the foot as a way to get attention from a neglectful husband. She laughed at that doctor and went home.

At that time I had graduated seminary and was serving my first church in Lebanon, Ohio. A young doctor and his wife had become my close friends there. One night when we were eating dinner at a local restaurant, I told him about my mother and asked if he thought her foot problem might be the start of Parkinson's disease. He told me to have my mother come see him.

She went to him the next day, and as I was getting into my car after a morning of vacation Bible school, she drove up. I could tell she was upset. The doctor told her she had some kind of neuromuscular disease and should go to Cleveland Clinic to be diagnosed. Later that day, I found out I was pregnant with my first child.

A few weeks later, my mom and I went to Cleveland, and within a few hours we were told that she had a disease called amyotrophic lateral sclerosis, or ALS. It is also called Lou Gehrig's disease because Lou Gehrig, the famous baseball player, had died from it. It's a rare disorder that causes the nerves in the brain and spinal cord to stop sending messages to the muscles of the body. My mother was told that her foot had been the first part affected and that the disease would move up her body quickly. First she wouldn't be able to walk, then she wouldn't be able to use her arms or speak. Eventually the disease would affect her diaphragm and she wouldn't be able to breathe. There was no cure and no treatment. They told her that people usually lived between six months and two years with this disease.

We returned home, stunned and devastated. Mom was forty-six years old. I told her that she needed to live at least nine months, because I could not give birth without having her in my life.

The disease progressed as we had been told it would, but it was moving very slowly. The sixth-month mark arrived and she was still able to walk. We knew then that she would outlive the six-month to two-year prediction the doctors had given her. She was still alive and in the delivery room during the birth of not only my first son, Julian, but also my second son, Britton, twenty months later. The disease was progressing, but it was much slower than anyone had imagined.

After about four years, Mom could no longer walk and was beginning to have trouble using her hands and caring for herself. It was highly irregular, but I asked my bishop to appoint me as the associate minister at my father's church so I could help him run the church and care for my mother. (In the United Methodist Church, the bishop appoints pastors to places where they feel their gifts and talents could best be used.) Much to my delight and the surprise of everyone around me, the bishop granted my request.

My husband and I moved to Hamilton, Ohio, and I began working side by side with my father. The church was small and could not pay me, so I volunteered my time and we stretched my husband's pay.

My mother was a brave woman. She never got angry with God over having a terminal illness at such a young age, and I never heard her complain about it even a single time. She faced each day with laughter and courage. She and my father were raising their grandchild, my niece Janell, and she set Janell's sixteenth birthday as the target for her death. She wanted to make sure Janell was old enough to be okay without her. If she lived until Janell was sixteen, she would need to live seven years with her disease. She was determined to make it.

Mom spoke openly about her death and made sure she apologized for anything she had ever said that hurt any of her family. She told us over and over again how proud she was of us and how she would miss us, but that she wasn't worried about whether we would be fine in the world without her. She made me and my siblings all promise to take care of one another after she died and to care for my father and Janell. She gave us her jewelry, bought us way too many gifts for Christmas and on our birthdays, and never let us leave the house without telling us how much she loved us! She remained positive, upbeat, and determined to live every moment of the time she had left on earth.

The only fear she had was of dying. She had no fear of life eternal or coming face-to-face with God. What worried her was the actual process of dying. Would it hurt? Would she know that she was smothering when her diaphragm stopped working? Would she die in her sleep or be awake?

Since I was her primary caretaker, she probably spoke more about her fear to me than to anyone else. I couldn't answer her questions, but I did share with her all the stories of the children I had been with as they died at the hospital. She had heard the stories when they unfolded. I called her after a death and told her in detail what had happened. She had been my confidante during my years as a chaplain. Now, though, the stories had added meaning for her. She wanted to hear them over and over again.

Hearing the tales of children who died peacefully and without trauma mesmerized her. I told her at least one of the stories nearly every day. After I finished, she asked me, "Leanne, do you think God takes care of adults like that when they die, or just children?"

I answered confidently, "We're God's children; of course God takes care of all of us! You don't need to worry." Then I silently prayed, *God, I have no idea if you take care of adults at their time of death like you do children, but I'm promising my mother that she has nothing to worry about. Please love and care for her at her time of death like you did the children in the hospital. Please, please, please! I am begging!*

There are lots of emotions that people experience when they're facing death. Elisabeth Kübler-Ross and others have labeled them as stages we all go through. They range from anger to denial to bargaining and then on to acceptance. My mother went through only two phases that I knew of. Most of the time she was accepting. I have a theory that this accepting attitude was the reason she beat all the odds and lived much longer than expected. She didn't waste any energy on being angry or trying to fight. She flowed with her disease, and her energy was saved for living. Plus she was determined to make it to Janell's sixteenth birthday.

The only other phase my mom experienced was fear. The closer death came, the more fear she had of the dying process. I could deal with nearly everything the disease brought. I washed and dressed my mother, fed her through a feeding tube, and helped her go to the bathroom. These were not always pleasant things, but I was determined to care for her the best I could. Her fear, though, haunted me. My mother was the strongest person I had ever known, and to see fear in her eyes would break my heart and scare me. I just kept praying my prayer to God, asking for her to be cared for as the children in the hospital had been.

Mom's disease progressed, and during the seventh year, just before her fifty-third birthday and a month before Janell's sixteenth birthday, she died. In the days before, we knew that her death was getting closer. Mom could no longer speak except in a whisper, and her words were slurred. She could barely move any part of her body except her arms a tiny bit. Her breathing had become shallow, and her body had become extremely thin as her muscles wasted away from lack of use. She was still able to sit in her chair and talk, but she was weak.

About three weeks before her death, she told me she had been composing a song in her mind. "It's the most beautiful song you've ever heard, Leanne! I wish I could move my hands just a little bit because I could play it on the piano. I know every note, and it's beautiful! I wish you could hear it." Sometimes she would even try to sing it for me, but her voice would not cooperate. The song delighted her. When she would talk about it, she would light up like a small child who had just been given a candy bar.

The day before Mom died, I was helping my best friend, Brenda, at a garage sale she was having. Mom called and asked if I would come over. She felt anxious and needed me. I immediately went to her, and when I arrived she was sitting in her chair watching television. She looked the same as always except she was covered with sweat. I went in and sat on the floor next to her chair. My being there seemed to lessen her anxiety. We talked for a while, then I went into the bathroom to get a wet washcloth so I could wash her face. I had no sooner finished than the sweat returned. I must have washed her face ten times while I was there.

Looking back, I realize that she was having what my granny used to call "death sweats." My granny had been a back-hills medicine woman and sat with the dying. It was sort of hospice care before hospice had begun. When I was a child, she would tell me about how people died and how she would know death was close when the death sweats began. But I didn't recognize them when my mother had them.

I sat with Mom for several hours, and then as night came and my dad returned home from the church, I told her I needed to go home. She reached out for my hand. I thought she was upset, but then she smiled and said, "Leanne, you know the song I wrote? The one I've been telling you about? I didn't write it. It's my song—my very own song! When you're going to die, the angels write a song for you, and you get to listen to it. Then when your time to die comes, you follow the music into heaven. I'm not scared now. I understand."

I started to cry, because for the first time in years, the look of fear that I had become so used to seeing was nowhere on her face or in her eyes. "I wish I could hear the song," I said.

"You won't hear my song," she replied. "When you die, you'll get to hear your own song of heaven."

I didn't know what to say, so I went into the bathroom and washed my face. Then I washed her face one final time. If I had known she was so close to death, I never would have left her.

As I started to leave, I kissed her and held her hand for a long time and then finally turned to go. I reached for the door and looked back at her, and she said, "The children were right! Thank you for telling me their stories, but now I have one of my own."

My mother died the next morning. My dad had given her breakfast, and she had asked to go back to sleep instead of sitting up in her chair. He propped up her pillows, kissed her goodbye, and went to church to lead worship. When he and Janell returned home, they found that she had died.

I was at the church I was currently serving when my mom died. I was seated in the front of the sanctuary facing the congregation, and one of the church custodians came up and told me that Janell was on the phone.

"Tell her I'll call her after church," I said, rather upset that the custodian was interrupting me during worship.

She looked worried and said, "No, you better come now."

It's odd, but my mom dying never entered my mind. I reluctantly walked to the phone and said, "Janell?"

She burst into tears and in a broken voice said, "Granny died."

I don't remember any more of the conversation. The next thing I remember, my kids and I were getting into my car. I wasn't crying. There was no time for tears. I just wanted to get to my mom as fast as I could!

When I got home, my dad was waiting for me in the yard. My good friend Lynn, who lived a few doors down from my parents, met me at my car. "Here, give me your boys," she said. "They need lunch, and they can play at my house until later. Call me when you want me to bring them back to you, okay?"

"Yeah. Thank you!" I said, turning to my dad and hugging him tightly. He held me close and we walked into the house.

My mother was still lying in her bed. As we waited for the coroner and funeral home staff to arrive, I washed her face and hands with a warm washcloth. I had spent the last seven years of my life caring for her and didn't know what else to do.

As I washed her face and hands and rubbed lotion on her skin, I imagined what it must have been like as she died. I could almost hear the music playing while her soul left its tired body and entered heaven. I could almost see her confidently and without fear walking into heaven and knowing exactly how to get there, because she was following her song of heaven.

I fell to my knees and said a prayer. I wanted to tell God how deeply thankful I was that my mom had died so peacefully. I wanted to thank him for allowing me the privilege of working side by side with my father, and for the bishop who had so sensitively appointed me to Dad's church. But mostly I wanted to thank God for giving my mother the song of heaven that had guided her so gently from this world into her life everlasting!

I had much I wanted to say to God, but only two words came out: "Thank you!"

14

Lessons Learned

A few weeks ago I was invited to officiate at the funeral of an eighty-year-old woman who had been a member of our congregation for her entire adult life. She had raised her children in our church, and her grandchildren and great-grandchildren still attend every Sunday. She was a musician and had sung in the choir, played the organ for our weekly chapel services, and accompanied the children's choirs on the piano until a year before her death, when she had developed dementia and could no longer keep her place in the music. Because of the dementia, she could not remember the days of the week except for two. She still remembered Sunday, the day to go to church, and Wednesday, the night of choir practice.

I was honored to give a eulogy in her memory. I ended it by telling those gathered that the Bible refers to singing in heaven several times, especially in the book of Revelation, where the heavenly beings sing beside the throne of God and Christ for all eternity. I told them that I knew beyond a doubt that this blessed soul would be right at home in heaven, singing, until we all arrived to join in someday.

After the service, I greeted people as they left the service, and a woman asked if she could speak to me privately. We walked over to an isolated area of the room, and she said, "When you spoke about heaven, I got this strong feeling that you really believe in it. I mean, you were so sincere and confident. What you said touched me deeply. You believe this, don't you?"

"Yes, I believe in heaven with all my heart and soul," I said.

I stood there alone for a long time. The faces of the children I've written about in this book streamed across my mind, and I realized that without meeting them, I never could have spoken about heaven with the complete assurance and confidence that I do now. I realized how blessed I was to be able to sit by their hospital beds and hear of the wonderful ways God cared for them as they crossed over from this world into the next. I thanked God for the lessons that each of the children taught me as they shared their experiences with me.

I had entered seminary wondering if I could ever speak of God, heaven, and life everlasting with the complete confidence that I had possessed as a child, after the doubts that had come with adulthood had crept into my mind. And here I was, nearly thirty years later, speaking with complete and utter faith about the world to come and the God whom we will see face-to-face when we arrive.

It wasn't a burning bush or mystical experience I'd had, but the truth, shared by children, that had renewed and strengthened my faith beyond any doubt. That small kernel of doubt that once haunted me so deeply is now nowhere to be found. The lessons the children taught me are lessons for all of us.

Lesson #1: There is life beyond death.

I'm not a scientist, and I don't know what happens chemically in our bodies and brains as they shut down. But I do know that the children I watched die were speaking or having visions not as a result of the drugs they had been given. Many times they were as lucid and awake as I am writing this book or as you are reading it. They were not "drugged-up kids" having visions. They were alert, playful, honest children telling me, and those around them, what they were experiencing.

James, Shane, and Jeffery went to church every week. God, prayer, and a strong faith system were part of their everyday lives. But other children such as Catherine, Joyce, and Tommy had rarely, if ever, been to church or had any formal religious education. All these children described heaven to me authentically and with their childlike honesty. They were not trying to impress me with their holiness.

They spoke of God, angels, visions, dreams, and imaginary friends as if they were an everyday occurrence, as if I knew exactly what the children were talking about, because they assumed everyone could see what they were experiencing. When Tommy spoke about "her" and described how beautiful "she" was, he would even get irritated because we couldn't see her. The children didn't believe that what they were saying would shock me or upset me or even comfort me. They were telling the truth, and I believed them. I have no doubt that there is life after death.

Lesson #2: Children are capable of very real and personal relationships with God.

I have spent my entire adult life working in the area of children's spirituality, and the one question I get asked more often than any other is whether I believe children are capable of really understanding anything about God, since they are not "old enough" yet. Those I have written about showed me that children can have deep and personal relationships with God. I watched them talk to angels, hear God's voice, and meet God in their dreams. They did not struggle to understand God. He was simply beside them, close to them, and a real presence in their lives.

James met Jesus on a bridge, and he spoke to James as openly and honestly as he would with any adult. Joyce had such a close relationship with God and trusted him so much that she was able to let go and stop her treatments.

At first I believed that children who were dying were special in their closeness to God, as if they'd been given an extra dose of holiness. I believed that they'd been given a spirituality other children hadn't. I had been taught well the old notion that you couldn't experience God until you had reached an age of intellectual maturity. But because my time at the hospital had shown me that children were capable of such relationships, I felt confident to ask children who were not ill about their relationships with God. I found that the majority of them also experience God in personal ways at a young age.

Through my nonprofit First Steps Spirituality Center, I now work daily with children who face all kinds of different issues. They struggle with the death of a loved one, the divorce of their parents, the deployment of a parent, the suicide of a sibling, self-esteem issues, being bullied at school, and many other hurts. I listen to them in much the same way as I did as I sat beside the children in the hospital, and just like those children, they tell me that in the midst of their struggles, God is very near to them. They see their loved ones appear in dreams, God comforts them by sending angels to watch over them, and they find the peace they need because of a deep and personal relationship with God.

Lesson #3: Dying is a uniquely gentle and personal process that we do not need to fear.

As I acknowledged earlier, the work of Elisabeth Kübler-Ross deeply shaped my life. She developed the five stages of grief and was one of the first people to write about the out-of-body experiences people have as they die. I had read her work and expected the children I worked with to move through the five stages, then to describe bright lights and the feeling of hovering above their own bodies as they were dying. I did watch them move through different phases, but it was not a one-size-fits-all experience. They were individuals, and as such their experiences with God were as unique as they were.

Rebecca saw a heaven filled with kittens and playfulness, while James met Jesus on a bridge in a green field. Shane was promised he could still care for his sisters after he died, and Andrew was assured he would discover the love he needed.

Some children, such as Jeffery, seemed to experience God only moments before they died. He saw his angel, spoke to him, and was gone. Other children, such as Jessica, who had her imaginary playmates, and Tommy, who had "her," spent weeks or even years with the angels that escorted them from this life into the next.

Catherine wasn't able to die until her father arrived, and Tony needed to forgive the man who had caused his death. God allowed them to hang on, to stay alert, and to make peace with those around them before they died.

As I watched these children, it became apparent to me that God knew them well, and because of that he knew how to help them move from this world into the next in a way that took any fear or anxiety out of dying. Tommy was a four-year-old boy who could not imagine life without his mother and who wanted nothing more than to stay with her. So God gently and lovingly prepared him to be able to leave this earth and enter heaven. God didn't take Tommy or force him to go; he helped Tommy by sending a loving presence to be with him and guide him home. God gently and personally prepared each child I worked with for their death.

Of everyone I had ever worked with, my mother was the most frightened of death. And then the music began playing in her mind. She heard heaven's song and was able to follow that music home.

Lesson #4: Heaven may be closer than we imagine.

As a child, I spent much time trying to figure out where God lived and exactly where heaven was. I imagined that it was far away and up in the stars. Many of the children I spoke to in the hospital feared death because they didn't want to leave and, as many of them would say, "be far" from their parents, homes, siblings, and pets. As God began preparing them for heaven, angels and imaginary playmates became part of their lives. Jesus met them in their dreams, and God spoke to them as if he were right beside them.

I often thanked God for sending the angels and for coming to the children, still believing that heaven and God's home were far, far away. But the more time I spent with the children and the closer their deaths became, the closer heaven seemed to be. And then, as they died, the process was much less dramatic and much simpler than I'd expected it to be.

Most of the education I had received about how people die was from television, where I watched while people gasped, made eloquent speeches as they died, and sort of sat up for one last time. Then there was the painful, fatal moment when they fell back, and someone would announce that they had died.

Death for the children was not like that. It was quiet, sometimes so quiet that we didn't know what had happened. I'll never forget Jeffery dying so quickly that it took all of the adults in the room, including myself, a few moments to even comprehend what had happened. Catherine died suddenly after her father arrived. I wasn't present for all of the children's deaths, but the one phrase I heard most often to describe them was that the child had died "quietly and peacefully."

It is hard to describe what being present at the time of death was like. The best word I can use to describe it is *holy*. There was a holiness, a sacredness, to that moment.

Sometimes the days leading up to a death were difficult. It was difficult to watch the teens with cystic fibrosis cough until they were exhausted. It was difficult to watch the cancer kids try to eat with huge sores in their mouths as a result of their treatments. Dying was not always an easy or pretty task. But at the moment of death, there was a holiness, a quietness, and a peace that in some way made it possible for those who loved the children to let go.

I had heard about Celtic spirituality for a long time but had never really studied it. A retired minister and his family recently started attending my church, and he is a leading expert on the topic. I asked him if he had a book I might read to understand a little bit more about the spirituality of the Celts. He brought me a huge box of books! I read the first one and then was hooked. I read every single one of those books.

Many things about the Celts resonate with me, but the thing that touched my soul most was their belief about heaven. They do not believe that heaven is a place in the clouds but rather that heaven is close to us. They describe death as a veil—a very thin veil—separating the living from the dead.

The Celts believe that dying is simply moving from one side of the veil to the other.

Reading the descriptions of those who die—crossing through a thin veil—was exactly what I experienced watching the children move gently from this world into the next. Death was simple. As I read that the veil that separates life and earth can be thinner at some times than others, it reminded me of what I had witnessed in watching the children relate to God in their last days. I had thought that God had sent those angels and had come to earth from a far-off place to speak to the children. But reading about the Celts, I began to wonder if perhaps heaven is closer than we imagine. Perhaps angels and God and the imaginary friends are with us all the time, and sometimes when we need them most, the veil that separates us becomes thin, and we see them, feel them, and know them.

Remembering that Julie, the teen with cystic fibrosis, had died and then appeared to several of the teens who had cared for her, I wonder if she simply moved the veil so they could see her. Knowing that Shane was promised he could care for his sisters even after he died, I wonder if he is simply behind the veil and closer to them than anyone imagines. I'm not sure where heaven is exactly, but I suspect it may be closer than we think.

Lesson #5: Death is a mystery.

These children and teens taught me many lessons. But one thing they didn't teach me was why death happens when it does. Hundreds of books have been written about the nature of God by authors trying to explain why bad things happen to people. Why children die is a main topic of discussion in those books. I won't try to answer that question because I don't know, nor did I have any great insights from the children that would answer it. What I did learn, though, was that God's love was very present as they died.

Many of the books theologizing about the nature of God portray his allowing children to die as his abandonment of or lack of personal care for them. The presence of God that I witnessed as these children died was not in any way a detached God who had forgotten them, but rather a God who was visible to them, loved them, and provided for their needs, gently moving them from this world into heaven.

I didn't learn why children die; that remains a mystery to me. I don't know why my mother died at age fifty-three or why my father had a massive heart attack twelve days later and died. I don't know why some of the people I visit regularly live into their nineties while begging God to take them to be with their spouse or children who have died before them. I don't know why my best friend died of cancer last year. There is, and I suppose always will be, a mysterious part of death. But one thing I know for certain is that God's love never abandons us, not in life and not in death. I watched God care for children in unexpected and wondrous ways. I watched him care for my mother as she died by allowing her to hear heaven's song.

I don't understand the mystery of death, but I don't fear it. Because of these children, I now sing the words to that old hymn with great confidence:

> And when from death I'm free, I'll sing on, I'll sing on;
> And when from death I'm free, I'll sing on.
> And when from death I'm free, I'll sing and joyful be;
> And through eternity, I'll sing on, I'll sing on;
> And through eternity, I'll sing on.

When I die, I'll sing on, and so will you!

The **Rev. Dr. Leanne Ciampa Hadley** is the president and founder of the First Steps Spirituality Center, which is dedicated to providing spiritual care to hurting children at no cost to the children or their families. It is also the mission of the center to provide training and workshops to adults who are interested in the spirituality of children and teens.

Leanne also serves as an associate pastor at First United Methodist Church in Colorado Springs, where she oversees and directs the children and family ministries. She is an ordained elder in the United Methodist Church and has specialized in children's spirituality for the past thirty years.

She is the recipient of Aspen Pointe's 2011 Hero of Mental Health Award, the Center for Christian-Jewish Dialogue's Dove of Peace Award, and the 2012 Lohman Award for her dedication to improving the lives of children.

Leanne attended Miami University in Oxford, Ohio, where she received her BA. She attended United Theological Seminary, where she received both her MDiv and DMin degrees.

Feel free to contact Leanne at hads14@comcast.net or visit the First Steps Spirituality Center website at www.1stSteps.net.

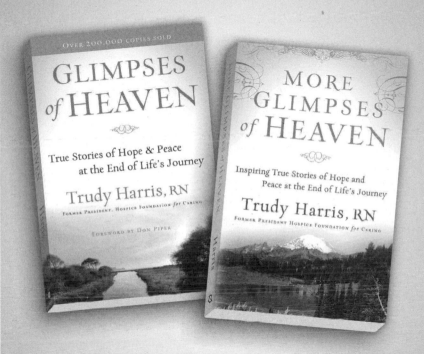